DEANN (WOLKOW) KRUEMPEL

Putting on the Big Boots

First edition

ISBN: 979-8-218-06162-3

This book was professionally typeset on Reedsy.
Find out more at reedsy.com

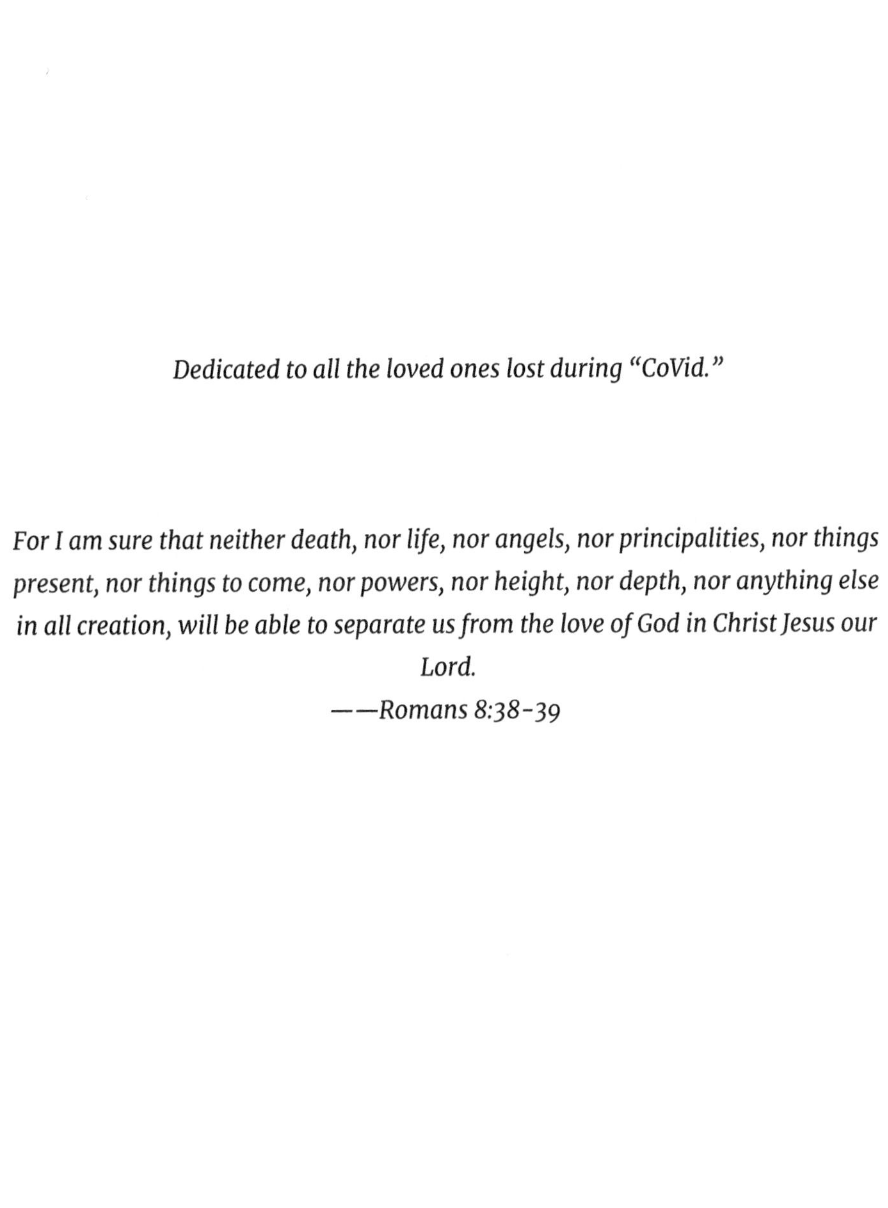

Dedicated to all the loved ones lost during "CoVid."

For I am sure that neither death, nor life, nor angels, nor principalities, nor things present, nor things to come, nor powers, nor height, nor depth, nor anything else in all creation, will be able to separate us from the love of God in Christ Jesus our Lord.

——Romans 8:38-39

Contents

Acknowledgement

My brother Delmer says we will never run out of memories. It is true that as I talk with my siblings more memories surface. From there new stories come forth, though each of us remembers different details.

I am truly grateful for all of the help from Deloris, Darlene, Dorothy and Delmer. Their input is just an email, phone call or text away. They add immensely to almost every story, and I feel closer to them because of our frequent visits.

Many times I wish I had asked our brother Don what he recalled about our growing-up years. Often I chide myself for not paying closer attention to the stories our parents told. It is not until we grow older that we realize the value of those memories.

The stories in this book were printed in several Midwest newspapers in 2021-2022 under the column name, "Putting on the Big Boots." (You know an adventure is about to happen when you put on the big boots!) The articles include a mix of memories and present-day observations, often contrasting the times.

Back in 2020 I wrote to the editor of my local newspaper and asked if he would print my stories to "help us get through CoVid." He asked me to send one. Thus began my first column, "Nooks and Crannies." Those stories have been published in *Once Upon a Midwest Sunset: the Nooks and Crannies Collection.*

Reader feedback is immensely rewarding. "Hey, I loved the one about—that reminds me of back when I was a kid and..." Suddenly, the hours spent struggling to get the right words all become worthwhile.

And the memories go on.

1

Stepping Up

Nancy Sinatra boldly proclaimed the purpose of her boots in her song back in 1966, "These Boots Are Made for Walkin.'" A. A. Milne's Winnie the Pooh stated that when you see someone putting on his Big Boots, you can be pretty sure an adventure is going to happen.

Growing up on our South Dakota farm, we often stepped into boots to get ready for the day's adventures—or the day's weather.

On frigid winter days when snow covered the yards, the men tugged on five-buckle overshoes. A soft coating on the inside helped insulate, adding another layer of warmth. The clasps secured the boot tightly around overall legs, keeping out snow and cold. Spring meant mud in the livestock yards. Overshoes slumped deep into the muck but usually kept shoes or boots dry.

Even in summer, chores required stepping into smelly stuff no one wanted covering their shoes. Two-buckle "rubbers" fit the bill, fitting snuggly over farmer work boots. Work done, the guys scraped off overshoes on the boot scraper, a metal blade that protruded from the edge of the sidewalk by the house.

When the day's adventure included mud puddles or winter cold, we all wore overshoes, even to school. Under the coats that hung on hooks in the back of the schoolroom, boys' and girls' footwear lined the floor, ready for recess.

The overshoes were made of rubber. Ultimately, holes or cuts happened and the shoes inside got wet. Bread bags provided perfect protection and helped the boots last another year. We stepped first into the bag, then pushed our plastic-covered shoes into the overshoes. No one minded if bread bags peeked over our boot tops.

Everyday work boots are critical for a farmer; feet need protection from falling tools and moving machinery, as well as the elements. Not only that, they need to last forever. Delmer remembers the day our father took him to Schmidt's Shoe store in De Smet to get his first pair of work boots. His eyes shined as he tried on the brown leather Red Wings, just like Dad's. When they got home, Delmer proudly carried the big box with the red feathery wing on top to his room. He put on the boots. Like a Coming of Age ceremony, the young boy suddenly felt like a true farmer, ready to take on the work just like Dad and Don.

Sometimes in life we try and step into big boots before we are ready. When I was five, I had a pair of red overshoes. Winter or summer, I pulled them over my shoes and socks whenever I could not run barefoot outside. One rainy spring day I was scooting through the yard trying to catch the newest feral cat. Dad looked out from under the corn planter in the Quonset and called, "DeAnn, go check and see if the cows have come up from the grove."

Behind the granary stood a tall wooden post from which we could see far out into the pasture. I hurried through the yard next to the house. Suddenly, I looked down at my red boots. I loved my little red boots. Last time I had climbed the looking post, I sank into mud almost up to the red buttons. Buttons held elastic loops that secured the top fold of the overshoes tightly around my legs. It was no fun washing the smelly muck off the red boots.

I peeked into the porch and saw Mom's four-buckle overshoes setting on newspaper. Mom wouldn't care if I wore her boots out to the post. Or, better yet, she would never know. I slipped off my shiny boots and stepped into Mom's overshoes. Even after I folded the top buckle back, large openings around my legs gaped up at me. My shoes flopped around inside like pinballs banging against a wall. I made such a racket clomping out to the granary the cows in the pasture probably heard it.

The overshoes sank into the mud next to the post, but I managed to wallow through. Mud-laden overshoes barely clung to my shoes as I one-footed up the fence. The cows were on their way home! I scrambled down as fast as lead boots allowed and stepped back into the mire. As I tried to turn, the mud held tight and my shoe slipped out of the boot and right down into the slimy black mess. Not thinking, I stuck my muddy shoe right back into the boot. I extricated Mom's overshoe with my hands and slogged back to tell Dad about the cows.

I felt mud soaking into my right sock and knew I needed to clean up Mom's boots. At the cattle tank I filled a bucket with the algae-green water. An old brush on the top of the tank helped scrub down the sides as I sloshed water inside, then poured it out. Finally, I washed my shoe and rinsed and squeezed out the sock ten times. I carried Mom's four-bucklers back to the porch, hoping they would dry before she needed them—wondering if she would notice.

Mom never mentioned wet overshoes, nor did she say anything when she sorted the laundry and found my one muddy-green sock. She never bleached it white either, which was unusual. I think she figured her little girl needed a reminder of the day she stepped into the Big Boots long before she was ready.

These old boots likely belonged to one of Mom's sisters.

2

Moving a Mountain

Twenty thousand years ago a glacier covered eastern South Dakota. On its amazing trek over mountain ranges, it broke off, moved and deposited rocks. The rocks varied in size and shape and mineral content, and much to the dismay of the farmers who came along hundreds of centuries later (and farmers' children), that glacier left a lot of them.

Every spring, like thistles, the rocks popped up from the fertile black prairie. Moldboard plows and field cultivators wrenched more stones up to the soil surface. Stones raised havoc with combines, pickers and planters, so when the menacing chunks of mineral dotted the hillsides and Dad announced Rock Picking Day; even the girls had to "put on the big boots." (I am pretty sure we complained, but we did so very softly.)

If the event occurred in early spring we used the hayrack or the "tin," a long sheet of heavy metal with a chain attached that hitched to the tractor. One of the girls drove the tractor, slowly pulling the tin sled or hayrack from one congregation of rocks to the next while the rest of the crew walked along, tossing on the larger stones. It was not possible to get them all, so we scouted for those bigger than a baseball.

When we reached the end of the field, we unloaded the rocks, one by one, onto a pile in the fence line and went back for another load. With each round, the pile grew into a bigger mountain.

My brother Delmer remembers often picking rock in newly-planted cornfields. The cultivator tended to push the stones next to the emerging plants. No farmer wanted to see rocks as he gazed down his perfectly planted rows. They needed to be picked. This work required the manure spreader and a skilled driver who could steer between rows. It would not do to wipe out an entire corn row. Occasionally, a young driver stepped up to the task and failed. After a few seedlings were flattened, Dad shook his head and called in a more experienced operator.

The soft soil worked against the walkers as we trudged over and between hilled rows from rock to manure spreader and back again. Even on a cool day the heat of the sun bounced back at us from the dark dirt. When asked about memories of rock picking, all four of my siblings responded with the words, "hot and sweaty." Even though the event occurred only one or two days every year, we were all relieved when the tedious, back-breaking work was over.

Of course, times change. Inventors constantly concoct contraptions to make life easier, and creating something to move rock was no exception. Mechanical rock pickers entered the farm scene. Tractors tugged machines that scooped up stones and tumbled them into a hopper that dumped with the flick of a lever. Farm youngsters breathed a sigh of relief.

Confucius once said, "The man who moves a mountain begins by carrying away small stones." That is what we did. Working together. One stone at a time.

On my recent visit to my hometown, I learned of another work-saving invention that makes rock picking obsolete—the land roller! Used mostly in young bean fields, instead of picking up the rocks, it pushes them back into the soil. In the fall when the farmer harvests his/her soybeans, no rocks or hard dirt clumps get thrown into the combine. Though not as memorable or as inspiring as moving a mountain, it does have its advantages.

Hmmmm. What will they think of next?

The rocks gradually moved from fields to fence lines or rock piles near home.

3

Never Throw in the Trowel

"We have to look at your garden before we go, Mabel." Summer guests at our home loved to see Mom's garden. It was beautiful. With a little help from the kids and Dad, Mom raised potatoes, beans, peas, carrots, lettuce, radishes, onions and tomatoes. A garden tour unveiled perfectly straight rows of lush vegetation in every color of green, which led the onlookers to the flowers. Tall spires of glads reached for the heavens. Dahlias as big as a dinner plate (Gurney's said so!) shimmered in the sun. Pinks, bachelor buttons, four o'clocks, nasturtiums, cosmos, rooster comb and Bells of Ireland bestowed the viewer with every color in a painter's palette. Yes, Mother's garden was a sight to behold.

When I was little, I beheld that garden often, always at Mom's side. I helped push in the two metal stakes that held the twine so that Mom could hoe a straight furrow for planting. I carefully spaced white and black bean seeds down the row, and Mom used the same hoe to cover them with soil. When I was five, I figured I already knew all there was to know about growing things. I begged Mom for my own garden.

The next morning, I dragged the hoe to the far end of the garden. My spot! I used the stakes and twine guide but discovered making the row straight was not as easy as it looked. I dropped in seeds Mom gave me, then covered them, pulling in dirt from the sides and tamping it down, just like Mom did. All the while, my imagination glowed with images of what my garden would look like. It would be perfect. Flowers of every color...Lush, green beans waiting to be plucked from the vines. Visitors would say, "Oh, DeAnn's garden is beautiful." I would pull up a few carrots, brush off the South Dakota dirt and hand one to them. We would munch the crispy orange roots while we basked in the beauty.

So, after planting, I pulled the hoe and row stakes back to Mom and waited patiently for my very own garden to grow. The next day it was not up yet. I decided it needed to be raked so that the seeds could come up easier. I pulled the garden rake over the row three or four times. Tiny furrows created by the rake teeth reminded me of Dad's cornfield. Surely the seeds would grow now. The next day—still no baby plants. I raked one more time just for good measure and because a leaf had blown down on it and then decided I should use Mom's garden cultivator. I pushed on the bar that was attached to the long metal handle that was attached to a bladed roller on the front of the machine. Five sharp tines just behind the roller dug into the dirt, loosening it and unearthing any weeds that dared show their nasty green heads. The cultivator, significantly taller than I, balked at the task (or the driver). Leaning into that handlebar with all my might, I managed to plow one swipe just next to the row, with only a slight chip to my front tooth.

The next afternoon, I sat on the grass next to my garden, willing it to grow. Soon I heard the mower and saw Delmer pushing the bulky green Moz-All back and forth in the lawn. The single wheel on the front swiveled my direction and I scooted away. When I came back, a light coating of slim grass blades littered one end of my garden. Glaring at my brother, I ran for the rake.

Not one seed managed to push through the soil in that first garden of mine. Mom smiled her knowing smile and simply said, "You'll have to try again next year."

Sixty-some years later I have a garden. Rows meander every which way and likely spill over with rogue radishes. Brome sprouts between the double rows of peas. A layer of grass mulch coats the space between rows. Last year's leaves flit from the compost pile in the corner and stop to rest at the base of a tomato plant. My garden is not perfect. I never offer guests a tour. But a few random flowers welcome the bees and butterflies. Mother Nature permitting, there will be enough tomatoes, cucumbers and beans for now and later. And last night's spinach-lettuce-kale-and onion salad tasted mighty good.

I'm sure thankful I didn't throw in the trowel back when I was five.

Mom loved her flowers from the garden.

4

Trapper Del and Cohort Go For Gophers

"Hey, DeAnn! Come help me. It'll be fun!" he said. When I was six I idolized my older brother. Seldom did he have to work too hard to persuade me to follow in his adventures, and this was no exception.

Last night at supper Dad talked about the burgeoning gopher population in the south pasture. "There's getting to be too many of them. They've killed the grass in a few places, and we don't need the cows and calves breaking their legs in the holes." He told Delmer he would pay him a nickel apiece if he trapped them. Delmer's eyes lit as he slathered butter on an ear of sweetcorn. Three gophers brought in fifteen cents. That was big money for a ten-year old.

So, the next afternoon Delmer and his cohort headed to the shop. He unhooked a trap with a handle and chain that was hanging next to the workbench. Next, he examined the metal rods in the corner next to the door, chose an old rusty one and handed it to me. "You can carry this," he said like it was a big privilege. At the water tank, he grabbed two metal buckets and dunked them in the tank. "You think you can carry it half-full?" I shot him my "I'll show you!" look and hefted the pail. He unlatched the gate to the pasture and opened it just enough for us to slip through.

I followed Delmer down the cow path because when we went through the pasture we always walked in the cow path. The gray South Dakota dirt puffed like powder in the hoof-carved furrow. It felt warm and soft between my bare toes as I tried to step in my brother's tracks. Wanting to see if I left toe-prints, I turned back to look at the path. Suddenly, I felt something different oozing between my toes, a wet, warm, grainy mass. I had stepped in a fresh cow pie! Of course, just then Delmer glanced back, awarding me with his silly grin. "Good job, DeAnn." (He always has been good at encouragement.) Then he wrinkled his nose and ordered me not to get too close.

At the crick a small trickle of water rippled among the stepping stones. Swishing my dung-laden foot in the tiny stream, I lost my balance, and the metal rod plopped into the water. My eyes shot to Delmer, praying he had not seen this mishap; thankfully, he trudged on.

Clinging to the pail with one hand, I knelt on the rock and fished the stake out of the shallow water. I ran as fast as I could to catch up but stopped quickly as my brother held up his hand. A striped, brown creature stood upright next to a loose mound of soil. Paws at its side, the gopher stood stock-still for two seconds, then dived down into a hole, emitting a bird-like trill.

Delmer rushed to the hole and motioned for me to hurry. By this time the water level in my bucket had decreased significantly. I lugged it to the burrow, hoping Trapper Del wouldn't notice.

I watched as he laid the trap on the ground. He stepped on the handle with one foot and held it down while he pried the jaws open with his hands and set the lever into its notch. A flat circle protruded from the center, attached to the spring. The trap was set. "Hand me that rod," he instructed. Then he pressed the rod onto the circle and the trap snapped hard onto the metal. "It works." Then he proceeded to set it all over again. "You don't want to get your fingers in it," he advised with brotherly wisdom.

Slowly he turned the trap over so the flat circle rested in the hole. Gently, he pulled the attached chain back into a straight line and pushed the rod through the wire circle at the end. That trap wasn't going anywhere. He reached for my bucket, only rolling his eyes a little as he poured the water slowly through the trap into the hole. All at once that trill sounded again ten feet away. The critter hightailed into the grass. It escaped through its back door!

"Come on. Let's find another one." (Trappers never give up.) This time, Delmer carried the bucket, and I dragged the trap and rod until we scouted another wretched rodent. Being fast learners, we knew we had to block the back door. Being a bossy big brother, he told me to put my foot over it. I narrowed my eyes. Pointedly, I glared at his sturdy shoes and then peered down at my bare, not-too-smelly feet. Obviously, he missed the point. He waited. I slowly lowered my tender, vulnerable little foot onto the hole.

He set the trap. I held my breath. Trapper Del slowly poured his full bucket of water into the hole. I imagined that gopher, frantically fleeing from the river of water rushing into his home, ready to bite anything in its path. I could almost feel the teeth clenching on my poor foot when, (SNAP!) steel blades shut with a dull clunk. "We got him!" the trapper whooped.

"It'll be fun!" he said. The next time I heard those words I was a bit more wary.

The next time we went gopher trapping, I wore shoes.

Delmer used gopher traps like this one.

5

Treasures of the Heart

She stood on her tiptoes to reach the highest shelf in the old wardrobe. Stretching far to the back, she carefully drew out a soft, towel-wrapped bundle. She carried it to the bed. I sat next to her, and at that moment I knew in my heart my mother was about to reveal something very special.

A gentle wistfulness radiated from her face as she removed the towel, leaving a soft wool bunting on her lap. She opened the pink flap to reveal a life-sized baby doll. The head was china, with brown hair, pink lips and rosy cheeks painted on the shiny surface. As she lifted the baby to her shoulder, I heard the tiniest click as the blue eyes slowly opened.

She smoothed the faded green calico dress with her fingers and finally spoke. Her parents gave her the doll for her fifth Christmas. Two of her sisters also received dolls and they spent memorable Sunday afternoons having doll parties. "I had other dolls, but they got broken. Sometimes the neighbor kids came over, and they were not always careful." She went on to explain that when the parents thought they were too old to play with dolls, they were expected to hand them down to the younger ones. "But I managed to keep this one."

I was thirteen at the time, and I knew the doll was one of the few tangible treasures remaining from her childhood.

Mom often shared memories with us kids as we were growing up. Even though she and Dad had to work like adults at a very young age, they still had time to play. When the folks married and had their own family, they realized the value of having fun.

My siblings and I did not lack for playthings when we grew up on our South Dakota farm. Don and Delmer "farmed" the living room floor, driving tractors, wagons and discs between chairs and under tables in the winter, then turning the sandbox into fields and roads in summer.

Deloris, Darlene and Dorothy all remember having dolls, a doll bed and buggy. Somehow our mother managed to find time to sew extra outfits for each doll, so we kept them dressed for every occasion. As in Mom's family, the toys got passed down to the younger siblings, so the toy boxes overflowed by the time I came along. As the youngest and most spoiled, I also had several of my very own dolls. One in particular, Susan, was extra-special.

Close to the end of my first grade year, the teacher gave the students permission to bring our dolls to school. The next day several girls carried babies around like little mothers during recess. Thinking I needed to be part of that group, I asked Mom that night if I could take Susan to school. She frowned and shook her head. "No, I don't think it is a good idea to take dolls to school."

Though disappointed, I left it at that, but the next day more dolls appeared. They got fed and burped and even had their diapers changed. So, again, I approached Mother. I pleaded. I begged. "ALL the other girls brought their dolls, Mom. PLEASE, can't I take Susan?" At last, she gave in.

The next day was great. Five of us carried our babies all over the school yard. They experienced merry-go-round rides and bounced up and down on teeter-totters. (A couple needed a diaper change after that!) Susan and I had such fun I couldn't wait to get home and tell Mom all about it. Maybe she would let me bring Jeannie tomorrow.

Then it was time for the ride home on the bus. Wrapped in a flannel blanket, Susan snuggled my shoulder as I one-stepped up the textured steel steps and took the second seat behind the bus driver. Bus rules stated that the younger kids sat in the front, high school kids in the back and the others in the middle.

I laid Susan down in the seat next to me, closest to the aisle. A boy my age sat in the seat across, and I noticed him watching. I unwrapped my precious doll and held her on my lap. I talked to her and showed her the sights as the bus began its journey. The boy kept staring at me as the bus drew close to our home. I put Susan back on the seat and reached for her bonnet. As quick as lightning, that boy grabbed her and swing her over his head with a wicked sneer. I yelled. The bus driver glanced up in his mirror and opened his mouth, but before he could say one word, my ten-year-old brother was there in the seat with that boy.

A scuffle ensued. I am pretty sure strong words were spoken, though I don't remember that part. At last my big brother handed Susan back to me. The bus arrived at our driveway. Bus Driver Clarence tugged the handle that opened the folding doors. His eyes met Delmer's as we stepped down, but there was no reproach.

With tears in my eyes I ran to tell Mom what had happened. As I looked down at my special doll, I discovered that her foot was broken. It had been partially torn off somehow during the skirmish.

We taped the foot on the best we could. Mom sewed a footed sleeper for Susan. It was a soft white flannel with tiny pink roses.

I still have Susan. She is wrapped in a pink wool bunting and tucked away in her sleeper with other precious things from my childhood. The doll is special to me, but the real treasure in my heart is the memory of that day in first grade when my big brother came to the rescue.

6

Sweet Summer Senses

Not a breath of air stirred that warm South Dakota night as I followed my farmer dad and brothers into the front yard. Through the open kitchen windows, silverware clattered and kettle covers clanked. Mom and the older girls were putting supper on the table.

As we stepped into the kitchen, hot, heavy air hit us like a blast from a furnace, but discomfort instantly turned to anticipation as a wonderful, enticing, aroma seeped into our senses. Sweet corn! We washed up quickly and slipped into our places at the table. Steam arose from the huge canner as Mom fished a dozen ears from the boiling water with metal tongs and piled them onto a giant platter.

Dad beamed as she set the plate of yellow goodness in front of him. We all loved sweet corn, but Dad enjoyed it more than any of us. Soon, creamy soft kernels, slathered with butter and sprinkled with salt, popped like cream-filled grapes in our mouths. Front teeth sliced off three rows to the end, then moved back to the beginning for another swath.

Bare, empty white cobs accumulated in front of each plate. Mom shook her head as Dad reached for another ear. She went to the stove to refill the platter. I heard Dorothy's soft giggle and looked up to see Dad add one of his finished cobs to Don's stack. Dad winked at me and I checked to see if Mom noticed.

For two wonderful weeks we delighted in sweet corn suppers every other night. At last, Mom decided it was time to put up the remaining corn in the field so that canned or frozen corn could also grace our table through winter months.

Everyone helped on corn-freezing day. We rode in the pickup to the end of the sweet corn rows, which Dad planted far from the sides of the field. I saw the four shorter rows growing between the taller, darker field corn and asked Dad why he planted them there in the middle. "The raccoons don't find it there, at least not as fast," he replied. "Raccoons love corn."

I happily followed Mom down one of the rows, a 5-gallon bucket clunking a rhythm against my ankle. A musky scent surrounded me. Bits of pollen sprinkled down like golden rain from the tassels, and velvety leaves brushed my face as I began this new adventure in the corn jungle. Mom turned to me then and sternly ordered me to stay in that row. "A little girl got lost in a cornfield a while back," she added, a worried frown darkening her eyes. I looked around me and could see nothing but stiff tall stalks and dark striped leaves in all directions. Just like that, the smell turned sour and stifling, and sharp leaves cut my cheeks as my imagination ran wild. I reached for an ear of corn and wrenched it off with a vengeance, longing for the safe open space at the end of the field.

With all of us picking and hauling, the back end of the pickup soon filled with a mound of husk-wrapped delicacies. Back home, we sat or stood next to the tailgate and stripped off husks and rubbed off silk until five boxes of golden ears remained. We threw the husks to the cows, who decided they were in heaven, and hauled the corn to the kitchen.

Mom and the older girls took over. Soon water bubbled in two canners. Mom slipped several ears of corn into each, timed it in her head, and then removed them from the kettle and plopped them into ice water in the sink. Once cooled, she and her girls carefully sliced off the kernels into giant bowls. I scooped the milky yellow tidbits into bags, sampling often to make sure it was good. Dad came in then and helped me carry the bags to the freezer in the porch. He smiled as he packed them tightly onto the shelf.

It was obvious that our father loved corn, not just sweet corn. In early summer he drove by the fields, admiring the straight, cultivated rows. Later, he parked the pickup at the end, crawled between the barbed wires, and walked out into the lush greenness. He came home, and with a twinkle in his eyes, informed his family that he could hear the corn growing.

Dad adored corn so much that some years, weeks before the sweet corn was ready, he presented us with an unusual gift. Delmer remembers Dad scouting through the regular corn fields and bringing home two dozen ears of field corn. He shucked off the husks and brought in the long ears for Mom to cook. Though not as tender and juicy as sweet corn, it still tasted good. As our teeth sank into the pale yellow morsels, Dad told how the field corn reached the edible stage faster than sweet corn. The problem was that, unlike sweet corn, the field corn remained in this soft, sweet stage for only one day (something about sugar turning to starch) before it morphed into rock-hard, tooth-breaking cow feed.

We asked our father how he sensed the exact day when the corn was fit to eat. He shrugged and said he just knew. It was a mystery to us; we speculated over his strategy. Surely there had to be some secret sign, some tip-off that revealed the magic day.

Finally, we decided it had to be the scent of the corn. After all, if he could hear the corn grow, likely he could smell it, too. Because Dad just loved corn.

7

The House That Kids Built

Rough gray columns of every size extended to the sky; cottonwood and boxelder trunks formed the walls on three sides. Patches of stinging nettle (I called them burning weeds) sharply jutted between the trees for added security. The ceiling was a canopy of green and brown, branches that softly swayed in the South Dakota breeze, lighting up the room with moving stripes of sparkling sunlight. For years, small feet pattered the ground there, wearing down the weeds to a floor of soft black earth. We called this space in the woods our play house.

Deloris, Darlene and Dorothy claimed the spot and made it their summer home when time allowed between chores and helping Mom. A square of plywood on a tree stump made the table. We sat on short log chunks pilfered from the wood pile. Peach crates and larger wooden boxes stacked along the walls served as the stove, shelves for dishes and pans, as well as beds for the babies. Tea was served in cans and chipped cups. Budding chefs honed cooking skills, baking mud pies and presenting them fashionably on paint pail lids.

I was not very old the first summer I followed two of my sisters to the play house. They likely would have preferred not having me there, but Mom gave them strict orders to keep an eye on me. Darlene opened the door, a five-foot stick that fit between branches of two spindly trees on the south side of the area. As she shut the door, I noticed four tall sticks leaning on a tree just next to it and figured they were weapons for fighting off wild animals and brothers.

Immediately, the girls got to work. Dorothy laid her doll, Dickie, in the biggest wooden box and reached for a battered, curved-bottom pan. She set it on the stove and turned on the burner, a bent nail on the side of the box. Darlene scooped some dirt into a coffee can from just outside the door and dumped it in the pan. Dorothy poured in water from a clouded jar and looked around for a spoon. A short dead branch hung within reach and soon became the stir-stick.

I sidled quietly over to the baby bed, sure that Dickie needed burping or something. "DeAnn, don't wake the baby!" (Sheesh!) As Dorothy stirred the mud-pie dinner, she looked around for something for me to do. "Mom sweeps every day," she said. "How about if you sweep the floor?"

I looked down at the powdery surface, scattered with boxelder seeds. "Why? It looks good to me."

The girls looked at each other with mutual sisterly annoyance. "We don't want it to look like a barn."

With a frown, I stared at the floor, thinking those little brown helicopters looked nothing like the brown stuff in the barn. "Why? I like the barn."

Dorothy stirred faster; probably the mix was burning. Darlene had an idea. "We need a broom. What can we use for a broom?" I shrugged, thinking I would rather take care of the baby than sweep anyway. "Hey! DeAnn, go find a bunch of long chicken feathers. I saw some in the yard by the coop."

As I reluctantly headed for the chicken yard, I shook my head and wished Delmer were not out in the field with Dad and Don. I could follow him around instead of hunting for feathers. But when I returned, the girls approved of my find and quickly twisted a piece of wire around the feathers at the bottom of a broken hoe handle. I swished it through the dirt and soon had a stack of twigs and 'copters in the corner. "Good!" Dorothy exclaimed and scooped some up with her hands to add to dinner on the stove.

Before we could eat (Thank goodness!) Darlene decided we should drive to Grandma's. Dorothy let me hold Dickie as we climbed into the "car," two old boards just outside, setting on tree stumps. Darlene sat on a rusty metal tractor seat in the front and drove us over the river and through the woods.

Over the years, four little girls spent many hours in that play house, making memories, creating, pretending and imagining. Though our parents often called us in after an hour or two, needing help in the kitchen or on the farm, they understood that children needed time to play outside on our own.

Today, child researchers expound the value of connecting with nature. They list advantages like better distance vision, absorption of more vitamin D, breathing fresh air, improved social skills and boosted learning. There is an organization in the UK, the National Trust, which lists 50 things children should do before they turn 11. Most engage the outdoors. One commends building a den or some sort of outside play area.

The Trust also recommends a "must-have" toy to inspire a child's imagination. They contend that this toy can become a pen, a broom, or a magic wand. (How about a door, a weapon or a spoon?). What is this magnificent must-have toy? A simple, humble stick.

Imagine that!

8

Gearing Up for What Mattered

Brilliant gold took turns with dark green on the rolling South Dakota hillsides; fields of ripening small grains lay between corn and alfalfa. The thin stems bent to the wind in glorious sun-kissed waves. Oats. Wheat. Barley. Every year Dad planted cereal grains, which ripened in early August.

The trouble was, hail could strip those amber waves of grain to bare brown sticks in a matter of minutes. Or, one torrential thunderstorm could leave them drowning in a lake of ruin.

Maybe our father had witnessed Mother Nature's random fury first-hand. Or, maybe the weight of paying bills and eight mouths to feed weighed heavily. Whatever the reason, Dad carried a sense of urgency into harvest.

Once the grain heads filled and dried, the guys checked the fields daily until they were just right to cut. On the day harvest began, Mom and the siblings geared up to the task. They realized how critical the time was and how much their help was needed. As the youngest and only ten years old, I sensed the urgency, but had no clue why it was necessary.

Usually Dad pulled the swather behind the John Deere 520. It cut and laid down the crop in a neat row, ready for the combine. Once harvest began, Don and Delmer drove tractors that pulled wagons to the field to be filled from the combine's auger.

The boys raced home faster than the tractor speed limit to empty the 100 bushel wagons. Mom hurried out to help the second she heard the tractor pull into the yard. The big green elevator loomed next to the granary, its spout inserted into the square opening on the roof. They pulled the trailer onto the hoist to lift the front end. Mom lowered the catch-hopper and cranked up the engine on the elevator. As the blades began moving, she pulled up the bar to open the end gate on the trailer. The tan kernels began their journey up and into the grain bin. I stood a few yards back taking in the scene, not minding the noise or the itchy chaff. Soon the wagon was empty and quickly carted back to the field.

In the kitchen, Mom and the girls mixed batches of lemonade and baked cookies. Sandwiches were made in minutes. Sometimes, Dad requested early dinner in hopes of starting the minute the windrows were dry of nighttime moisture.

One warm afternoon Dad needed another grain hauler. "DeAnn, you bring the 730 to the oat field right away." He showed me where to park and gave strict orders to watch him. He would wave when the hopper was full. I was to bring the wagon and get it under the auger as fast as possible.

I sat and waited as puffy clouds floated under the sun. Suddenly, a movement caught my eye. Something scurried from one windrow to the next, hiding in the grain-filled straw. Another shape followed the same path. Young pheasants flitted through the field, soon to be in the path of the combine's ravenous jaws. I had to do something! A quick glance at the hopper revealed only a tiny mound of oats, not quite full. Dad focused on the windrow. I scuttled off the tractor and ran to the birds' hiding place. They must have heard me as they scooted out toward the fence row. Just then three more feathered creatures appeared. When they hunkered under a swath, I tried to flush them out. Finally, the fifth bird glided into the safe tall grass.

I heaved a sigh of relief, then suddenly remembered the combine. Oh, no! Dad was off the combine, stalking toward me. I wasted no time checking for smoke coming out of his ears. I climbed onto that yellow seat and pushed the starter. I had never driven in any gear higher than second, but decided this was an emergency and pushed the lever into fourth. Ramming the clutch forward, I tore through the field. Dad was back at the combine, ready to flip the lever and empty the overflowing hopper into my trailer. The tractor hurtled in next to the combine. The wagon was directly under the auger. Dad flipped the lever and the oats poured out. The wagon sped by. I jerked back on the clutch as hard as I could, but I could NOT stop that tractor!

There was only a small mountain of oats on the ground as I circled back, finally having managed to stop and shift down. I stayed on the tractor as Dad shoveled the spilled grain into the wagon. I felt terrible, knowing I had caused extra work and wasted precious time and grain. Finally, the oats were transferred to the wagon and it was time to face the music. I climbed off the tractor, looked up at my father and said I was sorry. Hands on his hips, he huffed, "What were you doing, running around in the field?"

I told him about the little pheasants and that I couldn't just let them get run through the combine. He shook his head and started to climb onto the tractor. All at once he stopped and bowed his head. For several seconds he just stood on that step as I waited next to the wagon. Then he turned back and looked at me.

I swear I saw tears in his eyes as he spoke. "Did you get them all out?"

9

Just a Sunday Dinner?

A mother and father and their six children sat around a long kitchen table. A wren's cheerful song floated in on a gentle breeze from the open windows, providing background music. At a nod from the father, hands folded and heads bowed as the youngest said grace. The enticing aroma of fried chicken filled the air, blending with the apple-cinnamon scents that lingered from yesterday's pie baking.

The dad passed the platter of chicken and, as the household savored the Sunday dinner offerings, typical family chatter began. The father rehashed the pastor's sermon from church that morning, checking on his children's listening (or daydreaming) skills. Would the Yankees win the World Series again? What crazy stunt would their manager Casey Stengel pull this time? The father told how when he was a kid listening to a baseball game on the radio, fans went wild when Stengel tipped his cap and a bird flew out.

The youngsters smiled at the image as they ate. "Please pass the potatoes and gravy," the younger boy said. Then he added, "Good chicken, Mom." The mother smiled her thanks and soon the conversation turned to her childhood. She and her sisters peeled a huge kettle-full of potatoes so there would be enough for dinner and to fry for supper the next night. Milk gravy made with fresh cream was the best. It took three pies for Sunday dinner.

"Three pies!" one of the older girls exclaimed. "Oh my gosh, how did you have time to make three pies?"

"They probably didn't spend all their time talking to boys!" the older brother chirped. More teasing followed, finally hushed by a stern look from the father.

"I like bread best. I'm going to be a baseball player when I grow up. Do I have to eat my beans?" The youngest spread a thick layer of butter on her second slice of homemade bread and reached for the jelly. Siblings shook their heads, but made no comment.

Lighthearted banter resumed as apple pie was served. Even when finished, all remained seated at the table. At last, with a sigh of contentment, the father pushed back his chair, stepped to his wife and kissed her on the cheek. "Thanks for the good dinner."

The above scene is not part of a Hallmark movie. It is not part of a popular TV series. It was Sunday Dinner at our house long ago. Probably, it was Sunday Dinner (except maybe for Mom's amazing fried chicken!) in thousands of homes across the country. The TV and radio were off. No ringtones blared randomly from devices in pockets or flashing on the table. Actually, no one called at dinner time. It was common courtesy.

One short hour in our lives, but consider what took place. We felt special, so special that our mom spent hours preparing a feast every week, no matter how busy she was. We learned to be grateful for simple pleasures and how to express that thanks. As a family sitting around a table, surrounded by glorious scents and sounds, we communicated, face-to-face with words and gestures and facial expressions. We laughed out loud. We teased, but soon recognized the time to stop. Respect and thoughtfulness made it easy to be ourselves. No one interrupted or squelched even the youngest's contributions. Each person focused completely on the moment.

Back in the day, the idyllic noontime episode served as Communication 101. Has the tradition been lost? Replaced? We cannot stop time or go back to "The Good Old Days," nor would we want to in most cases.

It has been said that when we change the way we communicate, we change society. It doesn't take rocket science to see the change. Look around. Adults and children stare for hours at a tiny screen, ignoring those next to them. Thumbs get more exercise than any other part of the body. Human interaction cannot compete, so we stop trying.

Are we losing the ability to communicate face-to-face in the moment with words spoken out loud? Can we put on the big boots and make a difference in our society, each one of us? Can we make a change for the better?

Maybe bringing back "Sunday Dinner" is the first step. (Fried chicken is not a requirement.)

10

Clinging to Sweet Memories

Just south of the house a large cement tank extended up eighteen inches from the ground. A heavy round cover fit perfectly over the top. It took a lot of muscle to move the cover, but at a very young age, each of us was warned to never mess with that cistern. It was a deep tank that contained the water for our household use. During a heavy rain, one of the folks would step outside and pull the lever on the downspout that allowed rain water to fill the reservoir. When rain was scarce, we called William and Darlene, a dear couple from Erwin, and paid them to haul in a tank of water from De Smet. Though the cistern held a couple thousand gallons, a family of eight used a lot of water. Needless to say we never luxuriated in neck-deep bubble baths. As with everything else those days, we did not waste water on our South Dakota farm.

So it seemed a bit unusual one hot, dry summer, when Dad hooked up a hose and pulled it back to the garden. Carefully he soaked the ground around each of Mom's dozen tomato plants. "They need to be watered deep." He lugged in a straw bale from the barn and spread it under the plants to conserve the moisture, but every Sunday, unless it had rained, he watered those tomatoes.

Two months later, Dad helped himself to six tomato slices from a platter on our supper table. He spooned a generous amount of sugar from the sugar bowl on each, then sliced one in half with his fork. Juice dripped onto his plate as he lifted the first bite to his mouth. He closed his eyes as he savored the moment. The sweet goodness must have brought back memories of his childhood. For the next ten minutes he reminisced. As he spoke, we could feel his need to pass on precious memories of his mother.

She knew how to raise tomatoes. Even in the driest years, she managed to grow enough for their family of six sons and one daughter. As the round fruits turned scarlet, she would tug them from the vines and proudly arrange them on the old picnic table that sat next to the house in the shade. Each day she brought in a few to serve to her family with summer meals. When there were enough, she and her daughter Helen would pack them in jars and cook them in the huge canner. In plenteous years, jars of the red fruit lined pantry shelves to be used that winter for goulash, soup and scalloped tomatoes. But Dad's very favorite was his mom's wonderful tomato preserves on homemade bread.

Her name was Mary. She died when he was 17. Though many years later, we heard the emotion in our father's voice when he talked about his mother. We all listened quietly as we pictured this grandmother we never got to meet.

Summer breezes changed to bitter winds. Weeks passed and it did not seem long until we sat around the table laden with Thanksgiving bounty. Just before joining us, Mom brought a pint jar from the pantry cupboard. We heard the metallic pop as she used a table knife to break the lid's seal. She poured the red contents of the jar into a gold-rimmed glass dish and set it in front of Dad.

His hazel eyes grew misty as he looked up at his wife. "Tomato preserves?" He could only manage to shake his head slowly as he gazed at the special gift.

"It didn't want to set up," Mom apologized with her gentle smile. "It's kind of runny."

Dad lifted the spoon from the dish and let it pour back in. "Smells good." Then he reached for a slice of bread, spread butter on it and spooned on so much tomato preserves that it ran off the edge. He took a big bite. "Mmmmm. It's perfect. Just like my mother used to make."

Nearly sixty years later, I now understand why my dad used precious water to save those tomato plants. He needed to hold on to those memories of the mother he lost too soon.

As I sit here today, gazing at the variety of tomatoes lined up on my picnic table, I suddenly feel the need to make tomato preserves, the kind my grandmother used to make, the grandma that I never knew——My Grandma Mary who knew how to grow tomatoes.

11

Batteries Not Required

I couldn't find him anywhere! Mom had sent me outside to find Dad. He was not in the barn. He was not in the shop. I headed to the Quonset. The farm machines were parked neatly in their places along the walls. Only the John Deere Model 65 pull-behind combine had been hauled from its usual spot to the middle of the massive shed.

The soft, fine dirt on the floor muffled my footsteps as I padded through the steel building. I was about to go back to the house and report a missing father when I heard a merry melody pouring out from under the combine. All at once, three clangs added percussion to the tune. Dad was working under the machine and whistling!

He grinned when I told him Mom needed him and crawled out and set his hammer back on the workbench. With my hand swinging in his, I skipped next to him all the way back to the house, for a little girl must skip to keep up with her father as he whistles, "Skip, skip, skip to my Lou."

Our dad whistled. He whistled in the morning while he shaved in front of the mirror over the kitchen sink. He whistled as he tugged on his brown work boots and fastened the laces, getting ready to begin the day's work. The tunes varied according to his mood, the day, and recent events, but to me as a child, they always seemed like happy tunes. "Daisy, Daisy." "Take Me Out to the Ballgame." "Tell me the Tale That to Me Was so Dear." "Mairzy Doats and Dozy Doats and Liddle Lamsy Divey."

He whistled while he worked, but I think he had the idea long before Snow White promoted it in Disney's first full-length animated film. (By the way, the movie, released in 1937, was the first full-length animated movie in motion picture history. His wife advised Mr. Disney against the production, saying adults would not approve. For the first time in history, the wife was wrong. Ok, the second. I forgot about Eve.)

When he leaned his head into the cow for the morning milking and when he cleaned up after her with pitchfork in hand, a cheerful song emanated from his lips. One day I rode to town with him in the blue pickup and "My Bonnie Lies Over the Ocean" trilled through the cab. "Will you teach me to whistle, Dad?"

"Sure," he answered. "Anybody can do it. You just wet your lips and pucker them. Then you blow air through." I tried, and a soft tone came out. "Good. Then you move your tongue and mouth to make different notes. Then you practice. You'll get it."

Whistled tunes have been part of advertising jingles, movie soundtracks and television theme songs for a long time. Opie and his pa are obviously headed for a grand adventure as they march, fishing poles in hand, to the trilled tune, "The Fishin' Hole," introducing the Andy Griffith show.

It is said that this self-created music is a dying art; people just don't whistle much anymore. Some experts attribute the wane in warbling to technology. At any given time we can access music or games or some type of social connection with a touch of our fingertips. We no longer need to invent our own entertainment; therefore, we don't do it. Researchers also contend that lives are busy and noisy, and people fill them with other inputs.

Other experts extol creating music as a fantastic exercise for the brain. In this day and age, when more people seem to be worried about our brains and memories, maybe we should work on reviving the art of whistling.

There are no cables to connect. Songs are available on demand, right there in our brains. Batteries are not required.

Anybody can do it. You wet your lips and blow air through. You move your tongue and mouth to make different sounds. Then you practice. You'll get it.

Dad trying his luck at the lake. Likely he whistled softly.

12

There's Always Enough for One More

"They work hard," Mom said. "They need a good meal to keep them going." It was called dinner then and was the biggest meal of the day on our farm. Mom and her daughters prepared a "meat and potatoes" spread every day. She was adamant that the men be washed up and at the table at noon. After all, it would not do to serve watery potatoes or dry roast beef.

When farm work required extra helpers, like at corn-shelling time, Dad invited the workers to dinner. On those mornings Mom and the older girls bustled about the kitchen preparing extra food. At noon the men laughed as they ate, teasing Don and Delmer about mice crawling up their legs. The boys retaliated with a tale of the corncrib bull snake that made the old guys run.

Workers were always welcome at our big kitchen table, but the folks extended hospitality to others as well. If someone drove in the yard to ask directions and it was close to noon, Dad invited them in for dinner. Delivery drivers. The Fuller Brush guy. Mom never knew when a stranger might be sharing a noon meal with the family.

One day a salesman drove in around 11:30. Of course, Dad extended the invitation. "Come on in. There's always enough for one more."

Mom had fried pork chops that morning. She made a rich gravy, poured it on top of them and put the cast iron skillet in the oven. There was one pork chop for each of us. So when the man sat up to the table, Mom whispered to me that we would share one. I wasn't thrilled with the idea, but knew better than to complain.

Dad passed the potatoes around. Guests were served first. When the guy got the bowl of pork chops and gravy, he fished out the biggest chop, then poured most of the gravy over his potatoes. I frowned. Not only would I have to give up half my pork chop, there was no creamy gravy for my potatoes.

When Delmer handed the dish of carrots to the guy, he speared one small one, looked at me and remarked pointedly, "If we want dessert we have to eat our vegetables."

"Hmph," I thought as I noticed his rather rotund stomach pressing into the table. "I bet he gets his vegetables in carrot cake and zucchini bread."

For dessert, Darlene and Dorothy had peeled and sliced six Colorado peaches. Mom set the bowl of peaches next to Dad, along with enough sauce dishes for everyone. Dad passed the small dishes and the peaches to my brother. Delmer (obviously smarter than we gave him credit for) ignored the "guests first" rule this time and spooned his fair share of peaches into his dish. He passed the fruit on to the salesman. That man set the serving dish next to his coffee cup and proceeded to dump most of the remaining peaches directly onto his plate!

My mouth dropped open as I stared while he dug into dessert like a starving pig. I was about to say something when my eyes caught Dad's, and I saw them twinkle as he shook his head just a little.

After the guy left, Dad came back in to the kitchen. I told him what I thought of Mr. Hog-It-All. He ruffled my short hair. "Maybe he never had anything good like peaches when he was growing up. Maybe he went hungry when he was a little boy. We have plenty of food, and we should share."

I tried real hard to picture the roly-poly guy as a kid with protruding ribs and sunken cheeks. I felt guilty (sort of) for being so selfish.

Two months later on Dad's birthday, Mom made a special dinner with sour cream raisin pie, Dad's favorite, for dessert. She sliced the pie; there was one big slice for Dad and smaller slices for the rest of us, just enough for the family. We were almost ready to eat when we heard gravel crunching in the driveway. Delmer peeked out the window. "It's that salesman again!"

Dad walked outside and soon he and the Starved Kid Guy walked in and sat down at the table. Mom and we kids ate in silence while Dad and the man discussed the weather. At last it was time for dessert. Dorothy poured coffee, and I waited for Mom to bring the pie. I heard her shuffle things about in the corner cupboard. Finally, she placed a small serving plate of cookies on the table. They were iced oatmeal, the boughten cookies that she kept on hand for emergencies when we ran out of the much-preferred homemade ones.

As the cookie plate went around, the man craned his head to the counter and sniffed. He must have seen the dish towel draped over a pie plate but made no comment. He wrinkled his nose at the cookies, but still took two.

That salesman never returned, but plenty of other people sat with us at dinner on our South Dakota farm. Growing up we learned about hospitality and sharing with others. We learned that there truly was always enough for one more—well, almost always.

13

Signed, Sealed and Delivered

They have the power to tell love stories, fuse friendships and end wars. They can convey profound thanks, apology or heartrending regret. They can alter history. Words written on paper by a human hand—-letters.

In 1860, eleven-year-old Grace Bedell from Westfield, New York, perused pictures of Abraham Lincoln, presidential candidate. The girl decided that Lincoln's extremely thin face would look much better covered with whiskers. She wrote and told him so, adding that "all the ladies like whiskers and would tease their husbands to vote for you, and then you would be President." Lincoln wrote back to the girl, questioning the wisdom of growing whiskers, having never worn any, but shortly after their exchange he allowed his beard to grow. He won the election and began his inaugural journey with a full beard.

When families rode west in covered wagons, letters served as their only connection with the loved ones they left behind. Those journals provided permanent historical records as well as emotional ties to the person who wrote them. Knowing they may never see their parents, grandparents or siblings again, the words scribed on precious paper were a godsend in desolate times.

Not so many years ago, handwritten letters were still the main means of staying in contact with family or friends. There were phone calls, but whether thirty or three thousand miles away, you paid the long distance rate, and those minutes added up.

Young and old wrote letters from which relationships grew. Many marriages followed a stream of love letters.

Words on paper, specially composed for a loved one, staved off loneliness in trying times. A letter from home gave a young soldier the strength to carry on. Parents wrote to children who left home and were out on their own for the first time. Children wrote to parents, and the distance did not seem so great.

When we grew up on our South Dakota farm, the mailman drove up next to our mailbox at ten o'clock every day but Sunday. In the summer we heard the click of the metal door closing and the gravel crunching as his car drove on. Someone hurried to the mailbox and everyone in the house searched expectantly through the stack of mail. A personal letter generated excitement, whether it was from an aunt in Minnesota or a cousin in Sweden. Every one of us reveled in the words, which were the topic of discussion at that night's supper table.

I was five when my oldest sister Deloris went to business school. I missed her and I know our mother really missed her. Every week Mom sat down at the kitchen table and penned a letter to Deloris. I sat next to her, drew a picture and scribbled a few words on paper which she carefully folded and tucked into the envelope. She licked a five-cent stamp and affixed it to the letter. I ran it out to the mailbox and pushed up the "flag" so the mailman would know there was something waiting for him. Then I couldn't wait to get a letter back.

Dorothy remembers heading off to Bible Camp, her first overnight week away from home. Mom must have figured her daughter might get homesick, so she wrote letters. I wrote one too and signed it with my first cursive writing, "Love, Your Sister, DeAnn Wolkow." Dorothy still has the letter.

Years later when I went off to college, every day I peered into my tiny dorm mailbox, praying I would see a white envelope addressed by a loved one. Mom and my sisters often came through, and nieces added more cherished missives.

Throughout history letters have impacted lives. It's not just the words that give letters their power; it is the emotional connections. As we read the undeletable communiques written just for us, we picture the person. The words and stories come to life.

Songs on the radio testified to the emotional impact of letters. "Love Letters in the Sand," "All My Loving," and "Please, Mr. Postman" were just a few sung by Pat Boone, the Beatles and the Carpenters.

Today smart phones and computers allow us faster options for sending messages. A few seconds and the touch of a button, and a note travels instantly across the miles.

Is old-fashioned letter writing becoming a lost art, obsolete in busy lives filled with new technology? That depends on us. We can put on the Big Boots and keep this art and skill alive. It takes only a sheet of paper, a pen and a stamp. Our words may not alter history or affect elections, but they might stave off loneliness. They might impact a life. They might be a godsend in desolate times.

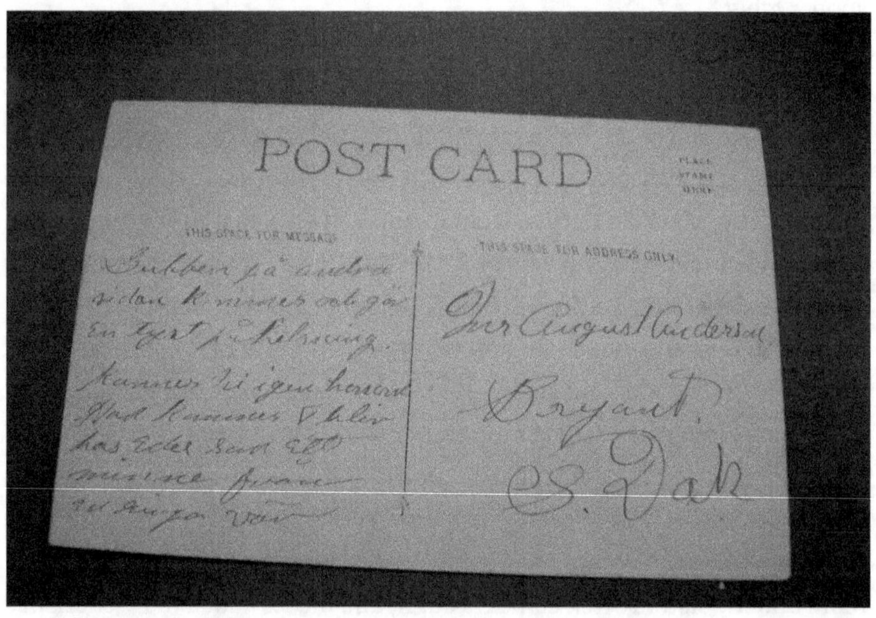

Old postcard written in Swedish. The sender's photo is on the front.

14

Heaven on Earth

"If cats don't go to heaven, then I don't want to go either!" I boldly announced to the young pastor at my first year confirmation class. Two summers ago I related this statement from my youth to three close friends as we sat around my sunroom table, while my cat Elsa rubbed tortoiseshell hairs on every leg and basked in the extra head rubs and ear scratches. "Of course they go to heaven," asserted one of the ladies. She smiled softly and added, "They give us a taste of heaven on earth."

One week ago we lost this dear lady. "Heaven on earth" seems a fitting theme as I consider her life. A bright, warm smile quickly brought strangers into her circle of friends. Likely, these no-longer-strangers found themselves sharing a meal at her dining room table within the month.

The woman loved plants, all kinds of plants, especially flowers. During summer visits to her home, one often enjoyed a tour through the gardens, teeming with flowing grasses and colorful blooms. One sunny spring afternoon I joined her in a walk through garden paths. Proudly she pointed out patches of different perennials, readily whipping off their botanical names. I nodded and smiled at what I hoped were appropriate times, not having a clue on the Latin labels. Chartreuse, heart-shaped leaves nearly covered the red bricks in one small area. The dear lady must have seen me admiring the soft green carpet. "That's Lysimachia nummularia." She smiled at the blank look on my face. "Creeping Jennie. I'll send some home with you." She hunted up her digging fork. One of the end tines was severely bent, but the bend did not hinder her digging, not one bit. I went home that day with clumps of Creeping Jennie and several other native plants which I tucked here and there into my primitive gardens.

The beloved friend also loved cats. They wandered among the trees and flowers at their home. Some met you when you drove into the yard. Others greeted you the moment you walked into the front door. Each of the pets had a story, and heaven-on-earth love shone in my friend's eyes as she regaled her fellow pet lovers of the many kitties she and her husband had rescued.

Three days after losing this friend, my cat Elsa died. Her death and the intense grief I felt in the ensuing days have been devastating. As I sat at my laptop, considering this story, I wondered for a few moments if writing about my loss was thoughtless, insensitive. After all, others I care about are hurting so deeply over the loss of their wife, mother, grandmother, sister and close friend. I thought of her and her love for cats, and suddenly I knew she would understand.

Last Tuesday morning I lifted the white box that held the body of my Elsa, hugged it close and carried it outside. Gently, I set it next to the serviceberry tree in the front yard. The tree canopies the graves of our family pets: Charlie, Heidi's precious Miniature Schnauzer and Cowgirl and Salty, Amy and Jennie's beloved kitties. At the other burials one of the girls had been with me, but this time I was on my own.

I headed to the garage for the shovel and digging fork. An image of a different fork with a bent tine flashed through my mind.

Tall spires of catnip and a carpet of chartreuse encircled the tree. The golden green vines were Creeping Jenny, the 20th generation of the same plants given to me by the beloved friend.

I pushed some of the leafy stems aside and reached for the shovel. The earth was cement-hard and dry. After removing the first few inches, I pushed the fork tines into the dirt, loosening another layer. Finally, the opening was ready. With another hug and many words of thanks for adding so much to my life, I placed my "Little Elsa" into the grave. My heart cracked a little with each handful of dirt that I pushed over the small casket. Tears mixed with the soil as I remembered all those we so dearly loved and lost.

At last, I gently patted the loose soil before me. I placed five red bricks over the mound in the shape of a cross. For a few moments I knelt there in silence. Finally, I stood and reached for the shovel and the digging fork. Suddenly, something moved in my peripheral vision and I looked down. As though brushed by an angel's wing, a bright-green sprig quivered and sprang around. The stem, covered with golden hearts, stopped and settled softly over the new grave.

I looked up and smiled through tear-filled eyes. "Yes, dear friend, you do understand. Give Elsa a hug for me."

15

Hi-Yo Silver! Away!

I don't remember a time when we did not have a television in our home as I grew up. The black and white Zenith sat next to the roll-top desk in the living room and often provided night-time entertainment for the family.

The enticing adventures that flashed on that gray screen drew me in far more than I care to admit now, as an adult. Already at the age of four I had favorite shows. The common theme was evident in my hero characters: Trigger, Fury, Flicka and Silver.

But our farmer parents believed there were far better things to occupy their children's time than TV viewing. "You don't need to be sitting in front of that television." I can hear Dad setting down the rules. When there was work to be done, we had better be helping. When there was time to play, we had better be outside.

I don't know if Mom and Dad had bicycles to ride in their growing up years, but they obviously concurred that their own children should have the opportunity. When Deloris was just old enough to ride a full-size bike, the folks wheeled one into the living room on Christmas Eve. She couldn't wait until the snow melted the next spring so she could ride it.

For a time Donald rode a russet-colored two-wheeler that Dad bought at a sale. When he was nine, Mom sent his name to a Sioux Falls TV station to be entered into their promotional contest, the Treasure Chest. During the nightly news, the anchor man drew a name for that night's key. Donald's name was drawn and his key opened the chest. He won a brand-spanking-new red Schwinn boy's bike!

My older siblings put many miles on those three bicycles. Of course, the boys rode the boy's bikes and the girls rode the girl's bike. (I never did get an answer when I asked why a girl's bike was different.) A short fender arced over the front wheel, a narrow tire centered on dozens of shiny spokes. Over the back tires on all three bikes extended a sturdy four-inch metal strip—the passenger seat.

One warm summer day Dorothy asked if I wanted to go on a bike ride. (Duh! Did the Lone Ranger catch bad guys?) My bare toes stepped on the chain guard, and I deftly swung one leg over and settled in right behind her. She sternly instructed me to keep my feet out, far away from the wheels. I nodded gravely, not sure why this was so important, but soon her feet pushed down on the pedals and we were off.

A soft, gentle breeze caressed my face. Gravel crunched in rhythm under the tires. Suddenly the metal seat beneath me became a smooth, brown saddle. Trees and grass blurred as we cantered by. Silver whinnied happily underneath us as we blazed a trail, onto the road and up the big hill.

We pulled back on the reigns and skidded to a stop at the neighbor's driveway, a quarter mile away. Silver's white mane flashed in the sunlight as he shook his head, turned around and galloped back toward home. Maybe in my wondrous imaginings I forgot my sister's orders and let my feet drop. Maybe I moved my foot to nudge Silver's flank. Whatever the reason, just as we were trotting into the driveway, I let out a shriek of shock and pain. My heel had been pulled into the whirling spokes. My sister braked immediately. She took one look at my injured foot, pulled me carefully off the bike and rushed to the house.

Dorothy felt terrible. She was crying when Mom met us at the door. They set me on the kitchen counter and lifted my foot. When I saw it I started crying, too! (Probably for all I was worth.) Dad came in and they examined the torn skin and flesh. They considered taking me to the doctor in De Smet but since there was no need for stitches, decided not to.

Mom filled a basin with hot, soapy water. Dorothy, still upset that her little sister was hurt, ran upstairs to get bandages from the medicine cabinet.

Dad stood next to me, his big strong hand resting on my shoulder. "Does it hurt bad?"

Opportune tears flowed down my cheeks. I sighed a long, pathetic sob, the big-breath shudder that happens when you have been crying hard. Then I sniffed a really big sniff for good measure and looked up into my father's worried hazel eyes.

"Dad, can I PLEASE have a horse?"

(Tune in next week for another episode!)

16

Pick Yourself Up, Dust Yourself Off, Start All Over Again

"Make sure she gets on the bike again," Dad instructed Dorothy after my heel was bandaged. We all knew what he meant; I needed to ride again to overcome the fear of getting hurt. In challenging life situations our father was known to say, "It's like getting thrown off a horse; you just have to get back on again." I was glad he didn't say that this time because he made it clear that I could not have a horse.

For a time I rode passenger when my sisters wheeled out the girl's bicycle. After the heels-in-the-spokes incident, Mom insisted that bicycle riders wear shoes. At first I clung to the handlebars, tennis shoes resting on the front fender where my heels were farther from the spokes. Eventually, I was back in the saddle, the passenger seat behind the driver.

When Delmer was seven, Dad brought home a 20" two-wheeler. "Road-master" glistened in silver letters on the wide red crossbar. Matching fenders extended from the bright red frame. The smaller wheels suited my brother perfectly. He stood on the pedals to power up hills. On downhill treks he sat, feet circling so fast the spokes blurred, pushing his bicycle beyond coasting speed.

Delmer fondly remembers his Roadmaster. "That bicycle changed my life. It gave me a sense of freedom." No more walking to the Quonset or the barn. Why walk when you have wheels? He even discovered an easy way to ride through the pasture. The gate between the pasture and shelterbelt consisted of three strands of barbed wire wound around several narrow four-foot posts. Delmer simply lifted the bottom wire, scooted his bike under, and then crawled between the lower and middle wires. In a jiffy he was trailing down the smooth cattle paths on his way to check gopher traps or take lunch to Don or Dad in the bordering fields.

Speed matters, and our father understood. He would give his son a shove on that bike to get him going even faster down the hill that led to the hog house.

As Delmer grew older, he ventured on longer rides. Probably imagining he was competing in the Tour de France, he headed out the driveway. No matter which way he turned, tall hills loomed, but flying wildly downhill like a car on a rollercoaster was worth the grueling uphill grind. After the four-mile jaunt around the section, he would come racing into the yard. Chickens kept an eye out for the Red Baron, ready to take a squawking flight to the coop.

If I was out in the yard, my brother would whiz right by me and slam on the breaks. The back tire stopped turning and gouged a furrow into the ground. Then we would examine the track left in the loose gravel and compare it to the last sliding, rock-crunching halt. Always in life it is important to better one's last endeavor.

On one of those show-off episodes, Delmer decided it was time for me to learn to ride. He may have felt bad that I never got the horse I wanted, or maybe he arrived at his strive-for-your-best philosophy at a young age and wanted to convey it to his little sister. Whatever the reason, he hauled the training wheels out of the shed and attached them to the rear bike wheels. I careened through the yard, touching down on one side wheel, then jostling to the other. It was fun to spin around the yard. I could even stop and remain seated without putting my feet on the ground.

I mastered steering, braking and balance (okay, two out of three). After the intensive, all-encompassing training session of maybe two hours, my brother decided I was ready. He removed the stabilizing side wheels and stood next to the bike.

"Okay, DeAnn, you can do it." Hesitantly, I swung one short leg over and tried sitting on the seat. The fact that the machine tilted dangerously to the left should have beeped a warning, but he straightened the bike and gave me a little shove.

I pushed down on the right pedal. The front tire wobbled. The wheels stopped turning. I crashed. The handlebar grip, the edge of the pedal and my left knee skidded in the gravel. Pain shot through my leg, and I just knew there were half-inch boulders jabbing into my skin.

Delmer stood the bike up on its wheels. I stared as he examined the entire left side. He carefully brushed dust off the pedal. He cleaned pebbles from the handlebar and peered in the hole at the end to see if there were any loose rocks inside. He shined up the "Roadmaster" decal with the bottom of his shirt.

Finally, he looked down at me, still sprawled on the ground, clutching my leg in excruciating pain. He grinned. "At least you didn't hurt the bike much."

I frowned. I looked pointedly at my gravel-infested knee. Blood oozed from three dark holes. Red scratch marks perforated the skin.

He gave a fleeting glance to my probably-fatal wound. "You'll be all right. Now try it again." He waited next to the bike. "Come on. You almost did it. You rode...(he measured the ground with his eyes)...almost five feet."

I stood up, wincing with pain. I swiped at the stream of blood running down my leg.

Did I ride again? Find out next week!

17

You Have to Keep Moving to Keep Your Balance

The gate to the front yard beckoned, only ten yards away. I pictured Mom inside the house working on supper. When I walked in she would take one look at my severely injured knee and immediately shift into motherly-care mode. She would gently wash the scrape and clean out the gravel. I could almost smell the hydrogen peroxide that she would pour over it, making it sting like the dickens. White droplets would puff out on all the scratches. "It's killing the germs," she would say as the tiny bubbles popped, whispering a fizzing sound.

I took one step toward the house. The broken skin felt tight as I bent my left knee.

"Wait, DeAnn," my brother pleaded as he steered his bicycle next to me. "Everybody tips over on their first try. Come on. Try it again."

I glared at the horrible two-wheeled monster that had bucked me off, causing me irreparable physical and psychological damage. I took another step.

"I'll walk right next to you all around the yard. You can do it. Come on, Sis. Get back on."

I hesitated. He patted the bike seat. "Just think, DeAnn. When you get really good at this, you can go bike-riding with me. I'll ride Donald's bike. We can even ride on the road."

The silver "Roadmaster" emblem sparkled in agreement on the crossbar as Delmer flashed his braces-embellished grin. Suddenly, it did not look so scary.

I slowly swung my right leg over the bike. I put one foot on the pedal. "You have to keep moving. Otherwise you lose your balance." The handlebars wobbled back and forth as I pedaled around the gravel circle with my brother at my side.

Thus began the dynamic duo, two-wheeled adventures of the youngest Wolkow kids. Around the farm buildings. Through the shelter belt. Though always a few feet behind, I pedaled for all I was worth to keep up.

One day we both skidded to a tread-baring halt next to the windmill. "Wanna race to the hog house?" he challenged in competitive sibling spirit.

I stared pointedly at his wheels that were way bigger than mine. "That's hardly fair," I retorted as I scoped the gravel trail down to the hog house.

"I'll give you a head start. Ten yards."

I shook my head. I was four years younger, but I wasn't stupid. "To the new granary."

"That's half way there!" (Even with giving me a head start, he didn't want to be beaten by his little sister.)

I shrugged nonchalantly, then with a mischievous grin, I pushed off and raced for the granary.

In spite of the huge lead, he still beat me, but we kept riding—-every chance we got.

The sound of rushing water after a spring thunderstorm drew us to the crick. A quarter mile down the road, the huge cement culvert diverted the crashing white water from the neighbor's field into ours. My heart pounded as we pulled our bikes off the road and footed down the kickstands. The wild rapids beckoned. We scooted carefully to the edge of the culvert and sat, our feet dangling close to the splashing water.

Not every ride was filled with excitement and danger. Sometimes we decided to ride around the section, legs pushing hard on the uphill climbs and wind blowing in our faces on the high-speed sprint down.

Spring rides revealed financial opportunity. With a gunny sack tied to the back of Delmer's bike, we covered the roads within a three mile radius, scouting for glass pop bottles in the ditches. The two-cent per bottle refund added to our savings.

Bicycles allowed a quick trip "down south." We traveled up the hill on the gravel road for a half mile and then hit the bumpy dirt road. A recent rain made the trip more fun—puddles. The faster the ride, the bigger the splashes! When we reached the pasture, we parked the bikes, crawled through the gate and felt very important checking the stock dam. Snapping turtles splashed into the water when we disturbed their tanning session. We watched the surface for movement and bubbles.

Summers flew by and other modes of travel replaced our two wheelers, but I am glad I got back on the red Roadmaster that spring day long ago.

When he reads this, my brother will probably grin that same silly grin (minus the braces). For, as much as I hate to admit it, he and Elbert Einstein had the same philosophy: "Life is like a bicycle; to keep your balance, you must keep moving."

18

It's All in the Way You Look at It

It happens to every one of us at one time or another. We travel along comfortably and everything seems fine. Then, suddenly our life journey takes a curve so sharp that we feel like we've been flung off the road. The pain of sadness is so great that we want to crawl into a corner and cry. We long to do a life reset, to go back to the way things were a week, a month, or a year ago. We forget all about putting on the big boots.

At times such as these, if we are really lucky, something happens or someone comes along to help us get back on the path. In my case this earthy angel was a child, my two-year-old granddaughter I had not seen since she was born.

"Grandma!" she called and ran into my arms. My heart melted. Thus began a whole new set of adventures and a new perspective on life.

"Come on, Grandma, let's go!" She grabbed my hand. What other choice did I have?

We discovered milkweed pods, split open and bursting with fluff. After a detailed discussion of the very hungry caterpillar, we reached for a pod. Small fingers tugged out the softness, and three dark brown seeds fell. A soft breeze came along, wrapped them in its arms and lifted them high above us. "Look, Grandma! Up in the sky!" We watched as the tiny parachutes drifted away. Within seconds hundreds more balls of fluff filled the air.

"Look at the pretty flower." She pointed to the yellow and pink tendrils of a vining honeysuckle. "Mmmmm. Smells good." Grandma, Mommy, the neighbor's cat, the chickens and ducks also enjoyed the olfactory experience, whether they wanted to or not. A lilac, miraculously blooming this time of year, caught the child's eye. "What's that?" Big brown eyes sparkled when the child reached up for the purple spire.

A few straggler blackberries remained on the thorny vines. On finding one she plucked it off and popped it into her mouth. Her face turned up. She closed her eyes and smiled. "Yummy," she whispered. "Let's find another one!"

Every evening we picked raspberries. Bees buzzed around us, finding nectar-filled blossoms. "Oh, look at the bees! Bees make honey. Bzzzzz." A raspberry-coated finger reached for a gentle creature, but it escaped to a higher spot. Somehow her bucket always ended up with the most raspberries, possibly because every few seconds she emptied Mommy's bucket into her own.

Snack time is critical when you are two. Josie did not hesitate a second when asked if she would like apples and peanut butter. "YES!" When handed the apple slice with creamy goodness on top, she observed, "It's a sailboat!" She proceeded to lick off the peanut butter, (the sail) and hand back the apple. "More!"

Grandmas want to do special things with their grandchildren; making memories is important. Of course, I had a wonderful plan. Josie helped find sticks and branches. We piled them in the fire pit. I started the fire to make hot coals, and we went to gather the goodies we needed. Graham crackers. Marshmallows. Chocolate bars. Roasting skewers. Mommy and Grandma worked together while Josie waited at the picnic table. We roasted marshmallows to light-brown-crispy-edged perfection. We carefully slid them between graham crackers that we had lined with a section of chocolate. Mommy proudly held out the confection, the warm marshmallow oozing out invitingly. "Here, Josie, try a s'more we made just for you."

"I just want the choc-o-late."

Often, as we were walking (rather, running) through the yard or on the sidewalk at Grandpa's house, she would look up. "Oh, look at the pretty clouds. Oh, look! There's the moon! It didn't go night-night."

The time flew by and the granddaughter had to go back home, much too far away.

Last night as I walked through the yard, I found a wilted lilac spire lying on the ground. I picked it up, held it to my nose and smiled. I considered the life lessons I learned from the two-year old.

Sometimes you need to grab someone's hand and say, "C'mon, let's go!"

The simple things in life are often the most wonderful.

Savor the good stuff, and by all means make sure you share.

Always, always remember to look up.

19

Two Wheels Keep on Turning

Years passed. Our bicycles spent more time in the shed than on the road. Baseball practice, games and 4-H meetings replaced leisurely rides around the farm. Quite suddenly, there was a need for speed—and headlights.

My brother recalls the day we got off the school bus and saw the '62 Ford Fairlane parked in the middle of the yard. A wheel hung out over the trunk. It was smaller than our bicycle wheels and fatter. A shiny red fender curved over the new treads. Dad strode out of the house with a grin on his face, and soon he and Delmer unloaded the 250 pound machine, a 65 Cushman Highlander motor scooter. Another two-wheeler but with an engine!

Delmer says he can still smell the newness of the bike and the burnt-paint smell that rose from the muffler on his first ride. The eight-horse, single-cylinder engine fit behind the legs of the rider. To start it you pulled up the rubber-padded lever in front of the engine and rammed it down to the floor with your right foot.

Cushman scooters featured an automatic centrifugal clutch, which allowed the rider to twist the right handle grip to accelerate. Turning the throttle counter-clockwise or down, increased speed; a clockwise turn decreased it. Cushman claimed a penny-a-mile operation cost. (Retail price of gasoline in 1965 was 30 cents per gallon.) Toward the front of the "step through design" floor was a single brake. The panel had no speedometer or gas gauge, only a light switch.

The scooter was a dream-come-true for my brother, his "ticket to freedom." He could cover the five miles to baseball practice at Erwin in minutes. The single front headlight and taillight permitted nighttime travel.

The passenger "seat" was the space between the black vinyl driver's seat and the gas tank cover on the back. I loved riding with my brother, and the motor scooter broadened our horizons. On Sunday afternoons we could easily trek to Spirit Lake for a swim on the sandy beach. Often Delmer would tell me I needed to learn to drive the scooter. "Maybe you can have it when I get a car."

The machine provided a peer connection with friends who owned scooters or small motorcycles. My brother recalls one Sunday afternoon when he met another cyclist and they motored to Erwin, Badger and a few places in between. It was close to dusk when he started home on the Erwin-Bancroft road. With two miles to go, the bike sputtered and died. He rammed down the starter pedal several times. No luck. Delmer was devastated, certain that something horrible was wrong. He walked home, worried about what Dad would say about him racing all over the county.

Dad listened to the distress in his son's voice. With not a hint of reproach, he got up from his recliner and grabbed his cap. On their walk to the pickup Dad said, "Grab the gas can."

With gas in the tank and three stomps on the starter pedal, the scooter roared back to life.

Then came the October day when my brother decided I needed to learn to drive. The scooter leaned to the left, supported by a thick kick stand while he gave me a demo of the throttle. "It's simple. You just turn it counter-clockwise to go faster." I turned the grip both ways. "Good. You've got it. Now hop on."

"What if I tip it over?"

"I'll be riding right behind you."

"What if I wreck it?"

"You won't."

The first circle around the yard was a jerky combination of quick bursts of speed and sudden halts. I was thankful Delmer was behind me to put his feet out on each stop. Gradually I managed to keep it moving. Curves evened out as I learned not to wrench the handlebars. Finally, I made one pass around the yard feeling like maybe I could ride the thing—-someday.

As we approached the gate to the front yard, I felt the machine tip slightly. Delmer had jumped off! My heart pounded wildly as I tried to keep going. I turned too short, then over-compensated, but managed to stay in balance. I continued on the curve back to the gate and twisted the hand grip, intending to slow down and stop. I turned it the wrong way! Speeding toward the fence I panicked, hurtling even faster.

The front wheel collided with the double-scallop yard fence. I just knew that I had wrecked my brother's beloved scooter. He rushed to the scene and asked if I was okay. Then we checked the damage. A deep scratch lined the front fender, which bent to the tire.

Delmer ran to the toolshed. He fixed the dent, but the scratch remained. Though we tried to bend the fence wires back into place, large gaps persisted.

Our father never asked about the fence or the scratch, but I wondered if he had figured it out.

The next spring he talked to Delmer about buying him a car. "We'll trade in the Cushman. You won't need it anymore, and DeAnn won't be riding it."

I knew it. Dad HAD figured it out!

Delmer gearing up to his Cushman!

20

Are We There Yet?

Times change. Inventors strive to make our lives easier by saving work or alleviating stress. Consider how technology has affected the ways we travel. I was in my fifties when I experienced my first airplane flight, not at all prepared for the turbulence or ear popping.

Barely two, my youngest grandchild recently followed her mother up the boarding bridge onto a Delta Airline 459 Boeing for her first flight. Buckled in her special seat, she waited for the takeoff. As the plane hurtled forward and began liftoff, the child clearly expressed her thoughts to every passenger on the plane: "I just want out of here!"

Travel can be a challenge. Add a child or three or more and "challenge" becomes an understatement.

Growing up, our family did not take many long car trips, but when we did we entertained ourselves. The car had a built-in radio, but most often we listened to our parents talking to each other; there was a continual commentary on the crops or the health of the animals grazing in the pastures. As Dad drove along, we all checked license plates and called out the name of the state. Delmer and I kept a tally of the pheasants along the road. I remember counting the cars in a train as it rolled along on its tracks beside us. We were never bored, or at least we knew better than to admit it. About the time I started pestering my siblings or asking "how much longer?" Dad would chime in with "Do you know what direction we are going?" and follow with a course in Cardinal Directions 101.

At the time, gaming devices, iPads or smart phones were unheard of.

Twenty some years later my siblings and I experienced travel time with our own children.

The miles flew by faster when Dorothy's family counted "Herbies" (Volkswagens). They sometimes made it down to 49 "Bottles of Beer on the Wall" before Ed, the dad, yelled, "Stop!"

Deloris recalls that her husband need only press down the brake of the old station wagon when their children passed the acceptable noise and complaint limits.

Books, crayons, notebooks and travel games filled our vehicle when my family journeyed into the sunset. A cassette player sported the dash of our 1992 Dodge Caravan. *Psalty the Singing Songbook* entertained us while we cruised along. As the ride drew longer, the five daughters grew restless. Tattling began. "She's looking out my window!" (Seriously?) Their dad decided Psalty should sing louder.

On nearly every long excursion, the age-old problem occurred: morning orange juice coming through. Too far to the nearest rest area and too far to the nearest town, I remember waiting in slight embarrassment as I discovered why the grass is always greener on the other side of the exit!

Not long ago I had the opportunity to accompany a daughter and her family on a three- hour trek. Four boys crawled into the SUV and buckled up. They reached for their Kindles and phones and immediately became engrossed with the small screens flashing in front of them.

I leaned back on the comfortable headrest, thinking how good young parents have it these days with all the amazing technology for travel. No loud music blaring. No need to lug along crayons and notebooks and puzzles. No kids teasing or pestering each other. I settled in for a peaceful, relaxing drive with plenty of visiting time with my daughter.

About twenty minutes after merging onto the interstate, I felt feet press into the back of my seat. "Are we there yet?" We ignored the question, hoping a distraction might magically come along. "Mom, he touched me!" The daughter shook her head and looked at the dash, considering what country music station to tune in.

"How much longer until we get there? I've gotta go!"

I smiled to myself as my daughter rolled her eyes. Some things just never change.

21

Oh, Rats!

Two nights ago, just before dark, I discovered a big pile of loose dirt on the back side of the duck cage. Just next to the cage was a hole that led under and into the floor of the pen. Obviously, the chicken wire lining I had installed did not stop this critter. What worried me the most was the way the ducks acted. They did not want to go in. Even though supper (including Cheerios treats) awaited them in their small shelter, the web-footed birds avoided it like the duck-plague. Something had been in their home and terrorized them.

What horrible animal had dug the hole, and what could I do about it? Logic and past animal adventures told me I was dealing with a rat. Heart pounding, I crawled into the small house and shined the flashlight into all the corners to make sure nothing lurked inside. Then I filled in the hole from the outside and covered it with a piece of plywood.

As I strode to the garage for the live-trap, my mind skittered back to the long ago winter on our South Dakota farm, the winter of the great rat infestation. When you live in the country and have livestock and feed, it is a given that there will be rodents around. Our lab-mix dog, Rex and the menagerie of barn cats usually kept the population down to manageable limits, but one year the pesty, brown scavengers invaded the hen house. Beady eyes shone from corners of the coop on rare night-time egg hunts. Feed consumption spiraled but not by the eggers. Something had to be done. The men tried a couple of midnight raids with the 22 rifle but only managed to eliminate a couple critters.

Delmer recalls that finally Dad got the idea of putting one of the tomcats into the coop at night. Sprinkles (I take full responsibility for cat names) was a black and white, rub-on-your-legs pussycat. I couldn't imagine the gentle cat even stalking disgusting rats, say nothing about killing them, but I was wrong.

The next morning eight fat rodent carcasses were literally lined up next to the door. After a week of slumber parties with the chickens, Sprinkles was no longer needed as the mighty hunter of the coop.

Though the feline possessed amazing hunting prowess, he wimped out on standing up to the dog. One Saturday, a couple weeks after the cat cleaned the coop, we woke up to a six-inch blanket of whiteness on the ground. This was the heavy wet stuff that sticks to boots and shovels—and fur.

Rex bounced around in excitement about the new wet snow. He grabbed bites of it as he tore through the yard. The humans in the family added shoveling and scooping paths to our list of Saturday chores. No one noticed the slowly moving white form creeping next to the front porch. Rex had romped and rolled and pushed the cat through the snow until he was a snowball with tiny areas of skin and fur peeking out between hundreds of small ice clumps.

Just before supper, Delmer stomped off his 5-buckle overshoes and opened the screen door. He heard a weak meow and turned around to find the barely-recognizable Sprinkles, struggling to move.

Mom had a no-animals-in-the-house rule, but she also had a very soft heart. Sprinkles was soon sprawled on a rug in the warm kitchen as Delmer and I pulled and brushed packed snow out of his matted coat. After a couple hours, the snow melted and the cat began exploring the house. Mom and Dad both said "No!" to my sudden plea that we needed a housecat, so once Sprinkles was dry and fluffy, he strolled back outside to his role of rat patrol.

Back to my duck house this morning, I checked my trap for the second time. Nothing. I used smoked pork as bait, since I had leftovers in the refrigerator. In the past I have caught them with bacon. Maybe this guy is on a high-fat diet, so I will try bacon next. And maybe Cheerios.

Better yet, I wish I had a cat like Sprinkles.

22

But, Where Does It Come From?

It was Saturday night. The north windows trembled as they wrestled with the frigid November gales that buffeted our South Dakota farmhouse. The brown Siegler oil burner warmed the living room (at least one end of it) and some of the family settled in for a night in front of the black and white, ready to share adventures with Little Joe, Adam and Hoss Cartwright.

Mom pulled the battered aluminum dishpan (the same one she used to mix bread) from the bottom cupboard and set it on the table. She plopped a stick of butter into the white and red porcelain pan on the back of the stove. I went to the cold porch for the two-quart blue jar we had filled last week. By the time I returned, she had the black pan heating on the burner. I watched as she poured in cooking oil, measuring with her eyes.

She unscrewed the gray zinc lid on the jar, grabbed three kernels and dropped them into the oil. In a few seconds they sizzled and popped, almost in unison. Mother sprinkled more golden grains into the pan from the jar and secured the black cover. She smiled at me as she waited for plinking to begin. Pop......pop! Soon steam puffed from the hooded holes on the cover and wild clunking began. Mom reached for the red wooden knob on the top and began turning the crank with her fingertips. When the growing contents pushed the cover off and the noise subsided, Mom lifted the kettle from the stove, carried it to the dishpan and emptied the fluffy white-with-brown-flecked-delicacies. The whole house smelled of the heavenly comforting aroma. Popcorn!

When three poppers filled the pan, she poured the melted butter in a thin, even stream over the popped goodness. She gave it all a light sprinkling of salt and a stir as I headed to the cupboard for the bowls. It was my job to carry each heaping bowl to the crew in the living room as Mom filled them. Dad first. He made a great production of sitting up straight, sniffing in appreciation and thanking me. When the *Bonanza* theme song trumpeted, we were ready to reach for the crunchy white kernels, one at a time. We savored the warm goodness and licked the salt off our butter-coated fingers.

We had all shared in popcorn production. We knew where it came from.

Two weeks before, we had shelled the last kernels from their white cobs as we sat around the kitchen table. The pile of corn-coated ears dwindled as each of us used our own method to remove the yellow seeds. When thumbs grew raw from rubbing against the rough, dry rows, we tried twisting our hands against them, beginning at the bottom. Once there was an open place on the cob, the going got easier and the cob was soon empty. It took several evenings to finish, but Mom made sure we had a week between for fingers to heal.

Crank back a few months to spring...Dad led Delmer and me to the east side of the garden. Delmer was very good at planting the popcorn at our father's directions. I was very good at asking questions. "Why are we planting a whole bunch of short rows?" I figured it would go a lot quicker to make one or two furrows, drop in those seeds and be done.

"Corn needs to be pollinated," Dad answered. "When it doesn't get pollinated, the cob will be empty." Delmer plowed through the planting. I frowned in confusion. Dad continued. "Wind is a good pollinator. When the corn tassels, the wind brushes off pollen and carries it from one plant to another. Do you see why short rows are better?"

My brother pulled soil over the seeds with the hoe. He was on the third row. Again, I looked up at Dad. "Why don't we (I wonder if Dad noticed the "we" as I stood and watched) plant popcorn out in the field like we do the sweetcorn?" Dad explained that if popcorn got pollinated with field corn, it could be tough and may not even pop.

The three of us strolled back to the house and I felt a great sense of accomplishment at having planted all those short rows of popcorn that the wind would pollinate.

Nowadays, busy lives command convenience. It is far easier to flatten a package, pop it in the microwave and press a button. The aroma is enticing. It doesn't taste too bad, either; but as we hurriedly scarf down the entire contents of the buttery bag, do we even consider where that corn came from?

I just added popcorn to my next year's garden seed order list. I will have to put on the big boots to compete with the deer and rabbits who will want to raid the short rows, but it will be worth it. The grandkids will watch the plants grow, see the tassels brushed by the wind, and pick the husk-covered ears from the short stalks. We will shell the kernels off with our fingers and then pop them in my black, hand-crank popper. We will savor each buttery kernel because we will know where it came from.

The old crank popcorn popper is still in use today!

23

Blessed!

Our parents grew up during the Great Depression. Later, they experienced the rationing of World War II. Being prepared for lean times was a way of life for them. Though Mom worked next to Dad on the farm, she always managed to raise and pack away plenty of food for winter. Why buy it when you can raise it? Every little bit helps! Mother adhered to both philosophies.

Summer meals included bounteous fresh vegetables from the garden, but when there was extra, we packed it away. I remember Mom's proud smile as she carried two huge buckets of peas into the kitchen. Sometimes, even Dad and the boys helped split the pods and shell out the tiny green morsels. It seemed to take hours to produce a medium-sized bowl. Fresh peas tasted wonderful on those July days, and it took a lot to feed the crew. Still, Mom always packed a few packages in the freezer.

Weeks later, Mom and her daughters reached under the bean plants in the garden and gently tugged off the long, thin seed pods. Once harvested, all available hands worked to snip ends and cut or snap. In the kitchen sink we covered the cut beans with water. I liked to swish them around and then scoop them up with my hands and deposit them into quart jars via the jar funnel. Mom ladled in boiling water, added a teaspoon of canning salt and screwed on lids and rings. She carefully lowered each full jar into her four-quart pressure canner. A couple hours later, we heard the satisfying "snap" as the lid on each jar sealed.

At the end of the season, Mom left the final picking on the vines to dry. Deloris remembers helping Mom shell beans out of the pods one winter day. Mom simmered the shelled beans for hours in the heavy Dutch oven, then added bacon, onions and a jar of tomatoes and simmered them some more. The beans added a hot, hearty side dish for supper that night and several more meals to follow.

When tomatoes ripened faster than we could eat them, Mom happily got out the giant blue porcelain kettle. We dipped the tomatoes in boiling water, then quickly slipped off the skins and dropped the fruit into jars. After a few canning sessions, the basement shelves gleamed with jars, ready for winter chili, soup and goulash.

Our mother had a talent for making pickles. An aroma distinctive to each vegetable filled the house as cucumbers, carrots, beans and beets were transformed into sweet-and-sour treats to fill the relish tray for Sunday dinners and holidays. I clearly remember her pushing the butcher knife into a huge watermelon. She beamed as it split open with a crack. "There's a really thick rind on this one. It will be good for pickles!"

When harvest allowed, the men helped dig and carry in potatoes. Good years provided enough to be mashed, riced, fried, or rolled into lefse for the entire winter.

When branches bent heavily with small crabs and spotted red Wealthy apples, we helped Mom make sauce, apple butter and pickles. Later, she sorted the biggest and best to be stored upstairs. One fall night, the family sat around the kitchen table. Black ink stained our hands from the sheets of newspaper as we wrapped each apple and tucked them carefully into boxes. For months the stash stored in an upstairs room provided apple salad and Sunday pies.

One year Mom bought seed for Indian corn. Her blue eyes sparkled as she pulled back the crisp tan husks and arranged the colored ears into our Thanksgiving centerpiece.

It was a way of life we learned from our parents. They had lived through hard times, so they knew the importance of raising and packing away food. This explains why we worked to plant, harvest and store everything we could.

But what would explain the smile on our mother's face as she worked? I think she realized how blessed she was for what she had.

24

Lend Me Your Ears

Last night two pairs of headlights moved in and out of sight in the field across the road. Far into the night an engine whirred as the machine rolled back and forth among the hills and valleys. Every few minutes the lights of the machine rendezvoused with the other pair of lights—-the semi. Corn harvest. The huge combine plunged through twelve rows at a time, shredding the stalks and leaves, removing the golden kernels from the cobs, and then emptying them into the waiting truck. If I walked through that field today, my boots would crunch over pieces of stalks and leaves and bare red cobs.

Sixty some years ago, harvesting corn on our farm in eastern South Dakota was an "amaizingly" different operation. Dad drove the John Deere 520 tractor, pulling behind and beside it his John Deere corn picker and a grain wagon. Two rows of corn stalks fed into the snout on the picker. Snappers ripped the ears off the stalks and fed them into the rubber husking rollers. The ears of dry golden corn then traveled up the short elevator and flew out into the wagon. Delmer or Don waited nearby with an empty grain wagon. Once the picker filled one wagon, they unhitched the full one and hitched up the empty one. While Dad continued picking (sometimes into the night), one of the boys hauled the load home. Mom hightailed it out to the corncrib to help unload. Occasionally, they parked the old pickup close and shined the lights on the operation.

Months later, after the ears had dried, the kernels needed to be removed.

Claus the Corn Sheller Guy maneuvered his machine next to the corncrib. The end result (with a lot of help from neighbors and family) was bins full of shelled corn and a giant pile of corncobs.

We also had a hand-crank corn sheller for small quantities. We fed the ears into the hopper on the top and turned the long-handled crank. Strong metal teeth ripped off the kernels and deposited them in a bucket. The cobs popped out the side into a small pile.

The corn provided the winter supply of food for the livestock. The cobs. Well, the cobs provided much, much more.

Free and plentiful, they were fuel for cooking and heat. I can still see Mom's practiced hands scoop up a bunch of cobs from the basket and drop them into the round burner opening on the kitchen cook stove. They burned hot and fast, but she knew the proper formula for baking bread or cookies. On frigid winter nights, she would again lift the cover from the burner. To keep the embers burning longer, she also stuffed in a few sticks of wood. While we slept, the stove radiated heat.

Dorothy remembers when it was her job to bring in the cobs. She carried the wooden apple basket out to the cob pile, then hauled it back in, loaded with the rough, red ears. She learned the hard way not to forget to fill the basket. One night of filling it in the cold, scary dark next to the trees served as a good reminder.

Later, Delmer took on the task. Once or twice he tried to coerce his younger sister into helping. "Come on, DeAnn. You take this side." He pointed to one curved, shiny handle on the overflowing basket. Probably, he found it easier to do it himself than put up with the dramatic moaning and groaning of the spoiled youngest.

The room adjoining the shop served as a storage place for extra cobs. In case of blizzards or ice storms, there was always a dry stash closer to the house.

Corncobs warmed us in far more ways than one. My brother recalls trying to climb to the top of the pile, most often when it glistened with a blanket of snow. We laughed and fell as the narrow, red torpedoes moved and avalanched to the bottom.

When Mom and I read *Little House in the Big Woods*, she showed me how to wrap a cob in a handkerchief just like Laura's corn cob doll in the story.

Dad either had a talent for aerodynamics or he just loved having fun. One November evening after Mom plucked and cleaned three rooster pheasants (a successful hunt by the guys), he brought out his hammer and a big nail. He sent me to get ten cobs from the pile, "the longest you can find." First, he pounded the nail into the wide, soft white end of each cob. Then he pushed the shaft of a long striped tail feather into the nail hole—corn cob darts! We spent hours throwing the toys into the air and watching them twirl down to the ground.

In the old days corncobs were used in many ways. They provided heat and cooking fuel and sources of entertainment. They make good fodder for stories with a kernel of truth. What memories are popping into your mind? I'm all ears!

This old wagon carried many bushels of oats and corn home from the field.

25

The Wind Did It

Two days of sustained forty mile-per-hour winds. "Gusts up to fifty miles-per-hour," the weather radio droned this morning. "A wind advisory...." How long could it continue?

No excited quacking greeted me tonight as I rounded the corner of the house to do chores. Even the ducks hunkered down in their small shelter, avoiding the frigid northwest gales. The wind was still howling.

Dust and small debris filled the air and drove into my face. Something whirled in my peripheral and I looked up to see three long, thin corn leaves twisting and twirling, almost in formation. As I wondered if there would be anything left in the neighbor's field, the tan trio whirled out of sight, high above the huge cottonwood.

Chores done, I wrestled the door shut, glad to be inside. The wind roared through the windows and I remembered a different corn field from long ago and far away.

The blue Ford pickup bounced over the rows as we headed to the south end of the field. I stared out the window, searching for snatches of yellow on the ground. I thought I saw something move up ahead and I imagined the wild animals lurking on the South Dakota prairie.

Delmer drew my attention as he maneuvered the vehicle between rows. "Dad said to pick up all the ears we can. A lot fell off before he ran the picker through it. We can't let it go to waste."

At last he stopped and turned off the engine. We each grabbed a five-gallon pail out of the back and trudged through the rows of standing bare stalks. The full ears, often still covered in husks, lay in the dirt, thicker on the hilltops. We worked in silence, emptying full buckets in the back of the pickup, then heading back for more.

"How come so much corn fell off?" (I never could be quiet for long.)

"Dad said the wind did it. Remember that night a couple weeks ago when it blew like crazy?" Did I remember? The wind screamed outside the bedroom window. I imagined wild creatures trying to get in. Lions. Tigers. Bears.

My brother and I worked through the afternoon. When we covered a wide area all around the pickup, he drove it forward and we continued our search in the new area. When the back was full, we drove home and unloaded it in the corncrib aisle. Through the winter we would run small batches through the hand-crank corn sheller. The chickens would thank us.

Starting on our second load, we neared the end of the field. I noticed an area of black in the grass that grew in the fencerow. "What's that?" My curiosity and sense of adventure beckoned. I cautiously stepped closer to the massive pile of loose dirt. On the south side of the mound there was a huge round hole. My eight-year-old imagination conjured up creatures that might live in such a lair. Fearless Delmer walked right up to it. I stood behind him and peeked around.

"It's a badger hole," my brother replied. I wondered how he could be so sure, but he went on. "Badgers can be real mean. You don't ever want to get one in a corner." I frantically scanned the area for places a badger would consider corners. The barbed wire behind his den looked cornery-enough for me. Just as I was about to hightail it back to the Ford, Delmer yanked a big old cornstalk out of the ground and shoved it down into that badger hole! Seeing sharp white teeth and long, dreadful claws about to come charging out at us, I grabbed my bucket and ran.

My brother's wild laughter assured me that an angry, cornered critter had not eaten him. Powered by a surge of adrenaline I found a dozen more husk-covered ears. My imagination kept working, too, and my heart pounded as I emptied the pail and then fearfully glanced back to the mound of dirt.

All at once something whizzed by, dangerously close to my head. I screamed as it slammed into the bumper. An ear of corn bounced to the ground. I glared at my brother.

He hooted his distinctive Delmer-laugh and called back, "The wind did it."

I scooted to the other side of the pickup, just in case any more identified flying objects came hurtling through the air.

I picked up an ear of corn and wondered just how mean badgers really were. I pictured a huge, seething creature staring at the corn stalk that blocked his front door.

For just a second I hoped that badger might feel cornered.

The blue Ford pickup

26

Mmm Mmm....Ewww!

I nibbled the last bits of meat off the chicken wing and laid the bones on the edge of my plate. The skin and the crispy coating were my favorite, fried and seasoned to perfection. I used my spoon to scrape together the thick, creamy goodness that was left of my scalloped potatoes. Though at least forty bowls, casserole dishes, and platters invited tasting on the food table that day, I chose our mother's offerings.

It was the Harvest Festival potluck at West Bethany Lutheran Church. I sat next to Mom at one of the long wooden folding tables that lined the basement. She and Etta Mae, our neighbor from up the road, were discussing their hens and the recent price of eggs.

There was a rule at our house: "no dessert until you've cleaned your plate," so of course I passed by the dessert table when I followed Mom in the serving line. Now, only bare chicken bones remained on my plate. Expectantly, I glanced up at the dessert table just in front of the door that led to the church kitchen. I slid off the cold metal folding chair and grabbed my plate.

Some of the ladies were already in the kitchen, cleaning up. Laughter and clattering of plates and silverware spilled from the open window. I scanned what was left of the desserts. Oh no! Mom's apple pie was gone! I stared in disappointed disbelief at her empty glass pie plate. Only crumbs of flaky crust clung to the rim.

I really wanted dessert. There was one tiny sliver of pumpkin pie in a blue porcelain pan, but it had no whipped cream on it. Just a few slices remained of a white cake with fluffy frosting, but a thick layer of coconut coated the top. Just then, I spied a plate of cookies at the back of the table. There was a cut-out turkey coated with orange frosting, and a few store-bought sugar cookies with holes in their centers. But wait! Peeking out from under the turkey's tail was a golden, crispy-edged cookie with three dark brown bumps protruding from the top. Yes! My mouth watered at the prospect of a chewy, sweet cookie with chocolate chips melting in my mouth.

I carefully extracted it from under the turkey and scooted back to the table to enjoy my find. I climbed back up next to Mom and with a smile of chocolate anticipation, I bit into that cookie. Something was not right, but I kept chewing. All at once my teeth and taste buds hit the bits of brown. EEWWW! They were raisins!

When I was a kid, I detested raisins. Sometimes, Mom put them in turkey stuffing. That was just wrong! Sticky, sweet dried-up grapes should NOT go in savory stuffing. Unlike Mikey, the kid in the Life cereal commercial, there were quite a few foods I did not like. Asparagus and onions loomed on that list.

After checking in with my siblings, Delmer and Deloris agreed with me about asparagus. We ate one or two pieces because we were supposed to at least try the mealtime vegetable, but that was enough. Cabbage? Absolutely not! Not cooked, not fermented, not in coleslaw.

Popeye's pecs protruded the second he downed a can of spinach, but cooked greens held little appeal for the Wolkow youngsters back in the day. Even a pat of butter didn't help. We never heard of eating it raw in salads or sautéed with bacon.

We grew older. Times changed. The variety of foods available grew, and for some reason our tastes changed.

Today, I sprinkle raisins on my almost-daily breakfast oatmeal. Oatmeal-raisin cookies are my very favorite cookie. As for my siblings, every one of us now loves asparagus. Spinach adorns our spring salads and adds crunch to sandwiches. We love cabbage and toss it in soups and crock pot dishes. Coleslaw on the menu? Sauerkraut? Of course! And we'll take onions with that.

Why have our preferences changed? Was it the present-day hype about the health benefits of eating certain veggies? Was it new terminology, like "superfood," that changed our perspectives?

Or do we simply want to savor childhood memories, and we've decided that maybe, just maybe that stuff wasn't so bad after all? Chew on that!

West Bethany at its new location near De Smet, South Dakota

27

It's More Than the Tree

The tree was a sapling spruce. Dad cut it from the fence line in the west pasture. A homemade star of foil-covered cardboard sparkled on the top spire. Strings of popcorn and cranberries draped over the scraggly boughs. The folks clipped brass candle holders onto the tips of the branches. Twenty-four small white pillars nestled among the short green needles and waited. Dad carefully lit each candle, then nodded to Mom. She extinguished the lantern. On that Christmas Eve long ago, the reflection of the glowing candles sparkled in the eyes of a young mother, father and their small girl and boy. A sense of wonder surrounded them, and for three short, enchanting minutes they felt in their hearts that nothing could be more beautiful.

Years passed. Electricity came to the Midwest. On a frigid day late in December, Mom and the kids sat in the car in front of Nelson Hardware in De Smet. The wind pelted flecks of white into Dad's heavy wool coat. He reached for one of the cut trees that leaned against the building. He held it up and looked at Mom through the windshield. On the fifth tree she smiled and nodded her approval.

The tree was a six-foot fir. Dad and the boys fastened the trunk into the Christmas tree holder they had made. They poured water into the large coffee can to keep the needles from drying out. They carefully turned the bare spot to the back and tucked the tree into the corner of the living room. A wonderful, woodsy scent surrounded us as we decorated that tree. Dad slid on the topper, a clear glass globe with a spire that reached for the heavens. Long, thin bubbler lights extended up from green wires. We stared in amazement as the liquid in the glass tubes warmed and bubbles rose to the top in constant succession. The older girls lifted fragile colored glass balls from their cardboard cartons and carefully looped the string over green needles. Colored paper Santas and reindeers, a collection of ornaments brought home from school, soon adorned nooks and crannies. At last, Mom unpacked the tinsel that we had carefully laid on a folded newspaper the Christmas before. Everyone strung tinsel. Silvery strands glistened in the light of the bubblers. The tree seemed to flow with the movement of the air.

Dorothy remembers squinting her eyes as she gazed at the shimmering sight "to make the lights sparkle more." Six children and our parents admired our decorated tree that year. We decided that nothing could be more beautiful.

My siblings and I grew up and went out into the world. We established traditions and celebrated Christmas in our own ways. One family went to the farm every year, cut a tree with a special saw and brought it home to decorate. Others bought live trees in town or from tree farms. Some of us bought artificial.

Stars and angels topped the trees in our various homes. Lights of large bulbs glowed in blobs of red, green and blue. Swags of gold and silver garland circled the trees. Each year special ornaments were added, some handmade, some gifts from loved ones far away. Each year we loved our Christmas trees.

Families grew and so did our trees. Red and white iridescent ropes of garland wrapped them in furry warmth. Large glass balls bent branches. Tiny pointed lights replaced the big colored bulbs. Some flashed on and off. Color schemes developed. Young hands hung ornaments that grew in numbers with each passing year. Reflections of sparkling lights danced in children's eyes; tears of love glistened in their parents.' Each year we thought this must be the best tree we ever had.

Tonight, I contemplate the sight before me—my Christmas tree that once belonged to our parents. Three small pieces of tinsel remain twisted on inner branches and make me smile. An angel, a gift from a daughter, glows from the top with "candles" of light in her outstretched hands. Multi-colored mini-lights sparkle amidst the white-and-silver garland. Ornaments cover the tree. Some are the same that decorated our parents' tree years ago. Many were made by small hands. There is a paper Rudolph, his red nose colored haphazardly. And a candy cane of red and white beads on a pipe cleaner, the winner in an ornament contest. Cutouts of etched brass and framed photos whisper a greeting. Each holds a precious memory.

And so I remember....Christmases past....the reflections of wonder in a child's eyes.... loved ones we have lost but hold forever in our hearts.

On the upper right side of the tree a small golden angel revolves among the lights. The tiny chimes that surround her sing softly into the night. The word "Hope" inscribed in her gown sparkles clearly with every turn. Tears glisten in my eyes. Yes, I am absolutely certain THIS has to be the most wonderful Christmas tree ever!

DeAnn (holding giant peppermint stick) in front of our tinsel-loaded tree.

28

Oh, What Fun It Was

Black balloons for milestone birthdays were unheard of back when we were growing up, but nothing would have dismayed our mother on her special day. She embraced each and every December 1st with spirits bright. Another year, another Christmas to celebrate. So on December 2nd, a new and glorious morn, Mom merrily began her yuletide pleasure of decking the pantry with jars of goodies.

She had made a list and checked it twice and stocked up on festive fixings. On the first day of baking, mom got out her giant mixing bowl, packages of dried fruit, jars of red and green maraschino cherries, pecans, and cans of cinnamon and cloves. Soon the house was beginning to smell a lot like Christmas as three round cakes baked in the oven. "Fruitcake gets better when it sits," she said as she carried the round metal tins to the cold porch that night.

Then, like five ladies dancing (Hey, you fit gold rings into this!) Mom and her girls made cookies. We stirred and rolled and baked. Sugar cookies, ginger snaps, Swedish spritz, chewy chocolate chip, salted peanut, and filled raisin.

I called the filled raisin "meat grinder cookies." I cranked the handle first as the grinder pushed oatmeal through small holes and converted it into tiny particles that we mixed in the dough. More muscles were needed, so Dorothy took over next to grind the raisins for the filling. Mom rolled out the dough and we cut out circles, then carefully spaced them on cookie sheets. Once baked and cooled, Deloris and Darlene spooned a dab of filling between two rounds. Wax paper separated the layers of filled raisin cookies as they waited for Christmas in giant glass jars out on the porch.

Fear not the candy thermometer, for behold it brought forth wondrous fudge, anise candy, and peanut brittle—-much to Dad's, Don's and Delmer's comfort and joy.

The weather outside was frightful, but the fire was delightful as lefse baked on the stove top. Fruit soup simmered as pearls of tapioca thickened the sweet dessert, as close to figgy pudding as we would get. Another day, our mom heated the rosette iron in hot grease. She carefully dipped it in batter, then back in the oil. Soon delicate rosettes waited in a cake pan to be dipped in snow-white powdered sugar.

At last, Mother beamed with joy as her porch overflowed with yuletide treasures. There would be plenty for family, friends and visitors.

One Sunday night, the snow was falling, and we had all settled in for a long winter's night of watching the specials on the small black and white. Ed Sullivan strolled on the stage in his suit of blue. He flashed a toothy smile and announced a "really big shew." The orchestra tuned, the audience swooned. The lovely, talented Connie Francis crooned, "I'll be home for Christmas."

Not a creature was stirring. The crew was calm, enchanted by Connie's slightly-sad song. All of a sudden, visions of ginger snaps danced in my head. I slipped from the living room and into the frosty porch. Treats lying in wait tempted my tummy and I could not resist their heavenly scent. I reached for a jar. A thief in the night, I lifted out one molasses cookie. I carefully re-stacked the others to make it look full again. I could not stop at one, oh, no! I stood on a chair to reach the salted peanut cookies up on the roof, I mean shelf, top. Again, I snuck out one and stealthily set the jar back just the way it was.

In the cold dark night I savored those cookies, watching and waiting in case the porch door should suddenly swing open and I would be caught.

I had pulled off the heist, I thought at the time. So sixty years later, thinking about Mom's Christmas baking, I started to wonder if I was the only one who had gone astray. I texted my brother. "Hey, Delmer, did you ever snitch Christmas cookies from the porch?"

Joyful and triumphant, I could hear the "ho, ho, ho!" in his voice as I read his reply: "Of course! Mom didn't seem to mind when a few were missing."

Oh, the wonders and wonders of a mother's love...

Merry Christmas to all and to all a holiday filled with sweet melodies and memories.

Mom's Salted Peanut Cookies

1 cup white sugar

1 cup brown sugar

2 eggs

1 cup butter

1 ¾ cup flour

1 tsp. soda

1 tsp. baking powder

1 tsp. vanilla

1 cup salted peanuts

Cream butter and sugar. Beat in eggs and vanilla. Mix in remaining ingredients. Form into balls and place on cookie sheet. Flatten with a fork. Bake at 350 for 10 to 12 minutes.

29

The Story in the Chipped Cup

In the split second before the crash, a warning flashed through my brain. I am pretty sure I squeezed my eyes shut and waited for the sound of breaking glass, but it was not the glass that broke. Yesterday morning when I opened my cupboard door, a juice glass tumbled from the top shelf. It took a nosedive directly to the counter below. Unfortunately, my just-poured mug of morning coffee took the hit.

The coffee did not even spill, but on the top edge of the mug a new white crater glared at me. Small pieces of pottery dotted the counter top and floor.

I honestly grieved over my chipped mug. This was not just any cup. It had been given to me several years ago by a dear friend. It was shiny yellow with a black rim, base and handle. All around the sides small, striped honey bees protruded, as if lovingly collecting pollen from the painted flowers. Yes, this cup was special, and I chose it on mornings when I wanted to think of this friend who passed away a few months ago. My emotions had evolved from sadness to peace when I reached for it. But seeing the hole on the rim broke my heart, for I did not want to part with this treasured reminder of someone dear.

Suddenly, my thoughts poured back twenty-five years ago to a different chipped cup. My mother's. I was visiting for a couple days, and Mom put out her usual spreads for meals and between meal "snacks" several times a day. We used her gold-rimmed dishes because, of course, now I was company.

The first night, just before bed, I saw Mother reach for an old cup that she kept under the cupboard near the sink. It was an off-white ceramic cup, the squat, dime store variety. Its circle fingerhold was long gone, and there was a hairline crack next to the rough stump that remained on the side. A slight tea stain coated the inside, leaving a distinct line an inch below the rim. Mom placed her index finger over the inside edge while her thumb clenched under the broken handle. She poured in water, drank it, and then placed the cup back in its place on the counter.

I frowned, wondering why our mother needed to use such a dilapidated old thing when she had plenty of nice cups in her cupboard. "Mom, why do you use that broken cup?" I asked. Her blue eyes met mine, but a small smile was her only reply. "I will buy you a nice new cup," I offered.

She said that she didn't need any more cups. Then she added, "I like to use this one." At the time I thought she was simply trying to keep her others nice, to save them for company.

The bits of yellow, black and white pottery littering the kitchen counter drew me back to the present and the chipped mug I held in my hands. Though it is only a "thing," it holds a story, a story of someone dear. Precious memories I want to keep. I wonder if Mom's cup had a story in it, too. Did it remind her of her own mother in her growing up years? Or her sister she had lost far too soon? Had Mom used the same cup when she and her husband of 52 years enjoyed tea together? Was it a gentle reminder of leaner times and how blessed she felt for all the wonderful things she had? Did using it somehow bring her comfort and peace?

Finally, I placed my yellow chipped honeybee mug back on the cupboard shelf. I will choose it when I want to remember my friend. I will treasure the memories. The broken mug has a story. Most likely Mom's old chipped cup had a story in it, too. It only took me 25 years, a crashing glass, and my own chipped cup to figure it out.

30

All I Really Need to Know I Learned at Recess

"It is recess time, students. Please leave your papers on top of your desks." Pencils clinked into their slots. Eyes lit in anticipation.

"George (name changed to protect the innocent), remember you must stay in and write sentences." The teacher deftly pulled the five-line chalk holder across the middle of the black board. With a single piece of chalk from the metal shelf on the bottom, she neatly scribed cursive within the lines, "I will raise my hand for permission to speak in class."

George sat across from me and I glanced over to see how he was handling the news. Head bent nearly to his desk, he wrote in his spiral notebook. Numbers lined the whole left side of the paper. I noticed that he had already written in an "I" next to each number. I wondered how he could have done that so fast. He glanced at me with a grin and whispered, "Got started during reading time." I shook my head and rolled my eyes. Why would anyone be so dumb to waste recess time writing 100 sentences?

In a very serious voice, the teacher announced, "Remember, third graders, you are NOT to throw snowballs." A few boys groaned, but we all knew the reason for the snowball ban. A first grader got a shiner last week when one of the big kids hit him with a snow ball. Someone said it had a rock in the center.

At last we had permission to leave our desks. Shoes squeaked on the wooden floor as we hurried back to the coat rack. We pulled on coats and stepped into overshoes or rubber boots. Hats and mittens came next. Soon the clomping of boots was heard in the halls of Erwin School. We pushed down the brass bar to unlatch the double front doors and rounded the corner for the playground.

The boys converged on the swings. They tramped down the snow under each wooden board and soon legs pumped back and forth over the snow. Hoots of laughter and puffs of steam filled the air as they competed to see who could get the highest.

Mrs. Sprang had recess duty that morning. Her long coat came down to the top of her boots, which was a good thing since she didn't wear jeans under her dresses like we girls did. When we were in her second grade, she would help us with our coats and tell us that recess was just as important as class time. Today she smiled as a group of us gathered around her. Addressing each by name, she inquired how our studies were going. Soon she pointed forward with the bell in her gloved hand, careful to hold the clapper. "You girls run along and play now," she encouraged as she glanced at her watch.

We passed the merry-go-round and the teeter-totters. Finally, we stopped to gaze at a huge expanse of untouched snow. We looked at each other and shouted in unison—"Fox and Goose!" Yvonne took charge and we followed in single file, creating a huge circle path. Two of us turned toward the center and later two more until an X crossed the circle. We quickly established the "safe" zone at the center.

Nila volunteered to be the fox first. She was a fast runner and I knew I would soon be caught, but we ran around that circle for all we were worth until Mrs. Sprang rang the bell. Hurrying inside we made plans to continue at noon recess.

After lunch we were soon bundled up and outside again. As we negotiated who would be the fox, three second grade girls watched from outside our circle. We all remembered way back when we were little kids like that last year and invited them to play.

One girl didn't have boots and her worn saddle shoes kept slipping in the snow. By silent agreement, when we older girls were the fox, we ran slower to allow her to get to base. Her eyes sparkled at being part of our group, and everyone laughed and shrieked as we played.

Suddenly, the playground grew quiet and two tall boys sauntered over to our circle. We all huddled in the safe zone in the middle and stared at them. One smirked and started kicking snow with his boots, destroying the path.

Never one to keep my mouth shut, I yelled, "Hey, you stop that! It's our circle." The other kid reached down and grabbed a glove full of snow. I am pretty sure he was aiming at me, but the snowball hit little no-boots girl right on her ear. I was so mad I grabbed a clump of snow and packed it with the other mitten. I wound up and threw that snowball at those big mean boys—just as the noon duty teacher rounded the corner.

I did not say a word as I stepped out of my boots, unbuttoned my coat and laid my wet mittens on the heater at the back of the room. I strode to my desk, opened the top and grabbed my spiral notebook. I numbered down the left side, ending with 100.

31

No Question About It

Do you ever find yourself in a real jam where you can't make heads or tails of a nearby conversation? Modern-day jargon is a far cry from the way we used to talk. Once in a blue moon I will ask a grandchild just what a word or phrase means, but truth be told I don't mind admitting I was born long before yesterday, and sometimes, ignorance is bliss.

Back when my siblings and I grew up on our South Dakota farm, understanding what we heard was a piece of cake. Yessirree, Bob, back then a spade was called a spade.

The sparkle in Mom's eyes spoke volumes when Dad told her she was a sight for sore eyes. "That hits the spot!" he beamed after a swallow of her freshly-made lemonade. Mother blushed when Dad reminisced of courting days when he was sweet on her. Though he didn't know what she saw in him since he was still wet behind the ears and not worth a hill of beans, she stuck with him through thick and thin, and today they were as happy as larks.

When we were knee-high to a grasshopper, our parents clearly taught us a strong work ethic. From rise and shine to early to bed, we learned to knuckle down and do it right the first time because haste makes waste. If we put our nose to the grindstone, a lot of gumption and a little elbow grease helped make things go slick as a whistle. Once in a while we came up a day late and a dollar short. At those times, Dad was fit to be tied and we got the drift when he informed us we were enough to make a preacher swear.

Brotherly love was as bright as the clear blue sky, but the boys had their share of tiffs. "Want a knuckle sandwich?" earned the response, "You're cruisin' for a bruisin'!" Mom threatened to box their ears, but it was an idle threat because the rules were cut and dried—no roughhousing, at least not in the house. When they got older, each endured the other's smart-alec sendoffs amidst hoots of laughter: "No hanky-panky!" "Don't do anything I wouldn't do!"

Our parents firmly advocated a rounded education, which often included the fine arts. If we lipped off to the English teacher, we faced the music at home. The handwriting on the wall was as clear as glass; did they need to paint a picture?

There were four girls in the family, and at a tender age Dad felt the need to give us subtle hints as to what we should or should not choose for husband material, before we went head over heels. Of course, cheapskates and skinflints would not cut the mustard, nor anyone who was shiftless or dishonest (weasels lower than a snake's belly in a wheel track).

There were plenty of fish in the sea, so we didn't need to get smitten with the first guy who came along. Hold out for the cream of the crop. Smarts ruled the roost. A man could be a real looker, but still be a few links short—all brawn and no brain. We certainly didn't want to get hitched to a knucklehead bum or a total nincompoop or we'd be in for a rude awakening.

No bones about it! No beating around the bush! We always got the message, and at that time we thought it was just hunky-dory. Yes, words were simpler and easier to understand back when we grew up.

32

Heads or Tails?

"The cousins are coming!" That announcement invoked a sense of excitement in us, especially if the cousins were our same gender and close in age. Memories of ballgames and Anti-I-Over danced in our heads. We couldn't wait!

It was early June and the Uncle, Aunt and their four children from the West Coast would arrive the next week. Mom and the girls instantly geared into cleaning and baking frenzies. Dad, Don and Delmer mowed, trimmed and spiffed up the yard. Even the barns got special attention. Having company was a big deal at our house.

Our parents treated guests like royalty. They demanded the same of their children. When other kids visited, we were expected to let them choose the next activity. "You go first," we nudged with a nod, simply because they were company. Flipping a coin was never an option. So, a week later right after dinner, Delmer opened the sports cabinet and waited for his cousin to grab the preferred ball and bat.

Cuz scanned the contents, her gaze finally landing on the top shelf. "Are those boxing gloves?"

"Yeah, we hardly ever use them," Delmer brushed off the question, resisting the urge to grab his favorite baseball glove and run outside.

"Let's get down the boxing gloves." The cousin was insistent and the cousin was company. Delmer reluctantly pulled a chair over to reach the top shelf.

The four dark maroon gloves gleamed in the light. The soft leather-covered padding curved sharply in a fist shape. White laces hung from the underside of the wide, matching cuffs.

The kid whistled softly and brushed fingers over the supple, smooth surface, "These are so cool!"

"They're alright," Delmer shrugged.

"Let's box." Cousin said suddenly, sliding one hand into a glove.

"Uh, wouldn't you rather play ball or something? We got a new bat." Delmer stared hopefully at the other youth, who stood three inches taller. He was thinking this would be a good time to flip a coin, but hospitality must prevail.

The white nylon laces "zipped" as the cousin pulled them through the first eyelets. "Come on. Why don't you want to fight me?" A challenge flashed through narrowed dark eyes.

All gloves were laced and the two faced each other in the west corner of the front yard. The cousin pounded gloves together, impatient to start, then started dancing around like a pro.

No bell rang to indicate round one, but my eleven-year-old brother's heart pounded. He had a horrible feeling about what was about to happen. It was a no-win situation. Because this cousin was a girl.

She came at him, swinging wildly. He dodged an uppercut, then a right cross and a left cross. He wondered how long he could keep ducking when the inside of her glove glazed his left ear. At last he saw an opening. His left jab landed squarely on her nose. Pow!

She frowned and lifted the soft part of the glove to her face as blood poured out. The front of her blouse stained crimson.

The adults still sat at the kitchen table. Though she insisted the boxing match was her idea, all eyes swept to Delmer. Later, Dad gave him a strong talking-to about hitting a girl. It didn't matter that he was simply following the family rules of hospitality.

All-in-all, the cousin visit did not turn out the way Delmer had anticipated. Looking back, he wondered what he could have done differently. Even if they had tossed a coin, it would have been "Heads, you win. Tails, I lose."

33

The Best Winter Games

"This is a perfect night!" Delmer exclaimed as he slid the pasture gate open and let Rodney and Randy step through before pulling it shut behind them.

"Yeah, Dad said it almost got up to five degrees today!" Randy waited for the others with a shovel and an old broom standing next to him in the snow.

"Sure am glad it warmed up." Rodney adjusted his skates that were tied together and hung over his shoulder. "This is gonna be so fun."

The three, not yet teenagers, trudged through the cow yard. Delmer and the neighbor boys often visited each other's homes for the best source of entertainment. Tonight's adventure led them through the pasture where they followed the snow-packed trail the cows had made between rolling white drifts. A perfect round moon cast its light like a beacon over the whiteness. The glistening scene before them rivaled a Currier and Ives.

They covered the 700-yard walk quickly and soon found themselves gazing down the embankment to the stock dam. Two white ribbons curved over the blue-gray ice in the southeast corner where the South Dakota wind had left its signature. The rest of the surface gleamed clear and smooth as glass.

Scuttling between the deep, frozen mud holes left by hooves in warmer days, Delmer dragged the shovel down to the ice to clear off the snow. The other two hurried to step out of their four-buckle overshoes and into their black ice skates. Rod skated out with the broom to brush off the remaining snow. Delmer changed into his brother's hand-me-down hockey skates. Randy

96

pulled an empty soup can from his coveralls pocket. Let the games begin!

The game was their own invention, a sort of cross between hockey, soccer and kick the can. It was honed to perfection over a series of winter nights, where the moon provided the floodlight. The three agreed on goal lines at each end and plunked down clumps of snow as markers.

The tin can went in the middle of the rink. Only the kicker could score, and he had to get the can across the opposite goal line to earn a point. He could use the broom as a hockey stick if he wished. The other two served as goalies, trying to stop the can from crossing the line. Once they stopped it, they could push it back. If they could get it all the way past the far goal line, they earned kicker status.

Young boys quickly discovered that coveralls slid over ice nearly as well as skates. Layers of jeans with long Johns underneath provided excellent padding when skates suddenly lost contact with the frozen surface.

For nearly two hours the sounds of laughter, skimming skate blades and clanging metal rose in the moonlight and dissipated in the crisp, clear air. They played until the score was almost even, then exhausted, fell to the snow.

The youngsters lumbered back to the house; boots clomped at a much slower rate than before. Noses grew red and their breath puffed out in tiny clouds. The full moon followed as they approached the gate. Delmer unlatched the chain. "What do ya think, you guys? Wanna do this again next weekend?"

"You bet!" Randy flashed a grin and tugged his stocking cap down over his ears. Rodney nodded and pushed his skates back up on his shoulder.

"I sure hope it's this warm next week!"

34

The Lucky Ones

They were too young to go all by themselves, barely nine and seven. But their dad insisted they would be fine. The ice on the stock dam was probably a foot thick.

Dorothy tossed her blonde braids behind her back as she pulled on the woolen snow pants. "I can't wait to try my new skates!" Shiny metal blades laced with red leather straps waited on the floor. "I hope I can get the buckles on over my boots."

"I'll help you. They are just like mine," Darlene promised her younger sister. "Aw, Mom, do we HAVE to wear two pairs of pants?"

Bundled in layers from head to toe, the girls headed outside, skates in hand. She stood at the door and watched until they disappeared into the trees. She remembered her own childhood and considered how fortunate her daughters were. On the rare occasions when she and her sisters had time to play outside, they pulled on wool socks and boots under everyday dresses. Then there were those dreaded bloomers!

By the time she was Darlene's age, she helped with chores inside and out. Her brothers worked hard, too, but gender roles were clear. The boys in the family would go on to high school. The girls could finish eighth grade but then were expected to stay home and work until they married. Times had changed. She felt thankful that their children were growing up in modern times.

Almost two hours later, a dark cloud moved in from the west, and the woman started out on the snow-packed trail. The forecast said nothing about a storm. Back in 1940 the Armistice Day Blizzard came up so fast people and animals were lost. But the last decade marked huge advances in weather technology. She needn't worry. They were lucky; times were safer now.

Shrieks of laughter greeted her as she neared the embankment that looked over the frozen water. For several minutes she stood and took in the sight. Two carefree little girls, skimming (more like scraping) over the not-so-smooth surface. They "followed the leader." They raced. They landed on their backsides. More laughter——and they spotted her.

"Hi, Mom! Did you come to get us? We're not even cold yet." Darlene's rosy cheeks glowed just above her bright-red scarf. Both plopped down on the snow and unstrapped their skates, chattering happily. "Mom, you should come and skate with us!"

"I might break the ice!" Their mother's blue eyes twinkled.

"No you wouldn't! Did you skate when you were a little girl? Tell us about when you were our age." Dorothy looked up with a smile.

"I never had skates. Sometimes on Sundays in the winter we went outside and played on the frozen crick. We ran and tried to see how far we could slide in our boots."

She told them how she had to help with cooking and cleaning and taking care of the younger ones. When she was big enough to carry a bucket, she fed the chickens and gathered eggs. There wasn't a lot of time to play.

She walked to country school, even when it was bitterly cold. She wore dresses with layers of underthings. On stormy days, their Dad might hitch a horse to the bobsled and she and her siblings rode to school.

"You got to ride on a sled? Wow, Mom, you were so lucky!"

She remembered the bumpy ride in the rough wooden box on runners. She remembered frozen fingers and toes.

But one small mittened hand reached for her right hand and one clung to her left. Their arms swung together in rhythm with their steps as the dark cloud followed them home.

Mom just smiled and nodded. Yes, she was so very lucky.

35

Thinking Outside the Box

I stopped and stared. No! It couldn't be. There on an endcap in the seasonal card section was a very elaborate, sparkly, red and pink castle. Not just a castle, it was a castle VALENTINE BOX! The drawbridge lowered into an opening for depositing cards. It was complete, pre-decorated, ready-to-take-home PLASTIC.

Horrified that such a creativity-stealing atrocity existed, I considered parking my cart in front of it so no innocent child would set their heart on it. Maybe I could nonchalantly visit the bed and bath area and find a fuzzy towel to drape over it. What if I put it in my cart, strolled to the automotive section and suddenly decided I didn't want it anymore? More than once I had noticed that other shoppers must have pulled such a stunt.

No, I sighed to myself, there were probably cameras about, and I didn't want to worry they would put out a store APB at my next visit. "Attention, all associates. THAT woman is here again." I walked away wondering if times have changed so drastically.

I mentioned it to my nearly 102-year-old friend. "Kids love Valentine's Day!" she smiled and then recalled when she taught country school more than seventy years ago. On the Friday before the holiday, she brought a box from home that would become the class Valentine box. If you know this dear woman, it is easy to imagine a dozen children happily gathered around her. "Oh, that's perfect! Good job! This is so special." She encouraged as they cut red, white and pink hearts and attached them to the cardboard surface. For attaching purposes, a big glass jar of paste waited next to the project. A stiff brush protruded down from the cover and was intended for spreading. Fingers worked too, and a few youngsters could not resist tasting the minty-smelling paste.

I texted my siblings about their memories of Valentine's Day. All remembered making boxes to take to school (like little mailboxes) for the cards from the class. Dorothy decorated hers with paper doilies and red ribbon. It was a masterpiece! Delmer had a little help from his older sisters decorating his.

For my first Valentine box, I hunted up a shoebox, cut a slot in the top and wrapped it in white tissue paper. Mom must have seen me struggling for ideas. She soon appeared with a handful of lace and some large brightly-colored buttons. "Make it special," she said. And I did.

After the box was complete, I recalled selecting just the right Valentine for each classmate and writing "To" and "From" on the back of twenty-some cards. Then I penciled in the recipients' names and mine. The teacher had mimeographed a list of students, and of course, no one should be left out.

When I added candy conversation hearts, the selection process proved painstaking. I dumped the whole bag on the table and chose five candies to tuck in each envelope for the boys. It was critical to give the "S.W.A.K," "XXOO," and "Be Mine" hearts to just one boy—okay maybe two. I certainly did not want to give any others the wrong idea. Ewwww! For the girls I just dumped some in, knowing they wouldn't care what the candy said.

Yes, we loved Valentine's Day when we were kids. The time spent decorating boxes and preparing cards gave special meaning to the event. I couldn't help wondering if such a creative celebration continues today, in spite of our hectic lives and the availability of factory made ummm—-things. I texted my daughter, mother of a 7-year-old. "Is Jackson making a special Valentine Box to take to school for his party?"

"Yup!" she replied.

I sighed in relief. Kids still love Valentine's Day. And they're still thinking outside (and inside) the box!

36

Steps

The thump of my boots echoed in the cold, dark hallway. A bare bulb high above cast shadows over the old steps, but I didn't care, because when I got to the bottom of those steps and opened the door, an amazing world appeared.

Books! Floor to ceiling, hundreds of volumes lined the shelves. Titles on the dark-colored spines beckoned in gold, white or black letters. There was a distinct smell, not musty or old; it was the smell of books. I stepped in, imagining all the new worlds and adventures awaiting me right there in that room.

A quiet "hello" drew me out of my reverie. The librarian. She was not very tall and her shoulders hunched forward. In my mind she was old, but when you are eight, you think everyone over the age of 20 is ancient. She greeted me with a warm, understanding smile. I handed her the three books I was returning. "Did you like them?"

"Yes," I whispered, for such a wondrous, mysterious place demanded quiet. She deftly strode to the young people's section and pulled out four more novels.

"I think you will like these." I nodded, and she proceeded to pull out the cards, write on them and place them in a metal box. I breathed a thank you, clutched the books to my heart and stepped to the door. I wondered how this dear lady knew exactly what I loved to read every week.

Thirty-some years later, we walked up two sets of cement steps that led to a different library, several hundred miles from my hometown. Five little girls skipped up the steps with us, and we opened heavy glass doors. Inside were more stairs, one set leading up to the adult library and one leading down to the children's. None of us minded the steps, because in this big wonderful place there were thousands of books—beautiful, colorful books. The big wooden box, the card catalog, guided our searches. When we checked out, nice librarians wrote our numbers on the book cards and placed them in wooden files.

Another thirty-some years later that same library sports a beautiful "new" addition. There are no steps, except to the upstairs area, but an elevator makes even those unnecessary. Nice librarians are there to help. The online catalog is available at the touch of fingertips. After a quick scan of barcodes, happy patrons carry home books and other media.

For thirty years I have had the privilege of working at this library. As of February 4, retirement is my new chapter. Thanks to all of you who have been part of my library family through the years. Words cannot express the joy of reading to the second generation of story time children, with proud parents looking on. Thank you to the dear people who prepared such a memorable retirement party and all who wish me well.

Working with books, book lovers and children has to be the best job in the world. There are the adults who love the stories and want to keep their minds working. The youngsters who are drawn into the written adventures. The parents who read to their little ones each and every day. Lots of smiles happen in libraries!

Times are changing, though, and libraries struggle to remain viable. Fewer people come in. Fewer books are checked out. Why? It's the question I ask myself and others nearly every day of my life. The answer most often given: It is difficult to compete with plastic screens and instant-gratification games.

Statistics show that children who have been read to and continue reading on their own score higher than 90% on standardized tests. If fewer children embrace reading, will test scores plummet? Are we going to allow this to happen? What can we do?

Let's make sure that apps do not replace laps. A special closeness exists when an adult reads to a child, conveying an unmistakable message: You are so important to me that I want to share this time, and you will learn to love reading as much as I do.

Let's put on the Big Boots, America, and make a difference! Keep visiting our libraries (or start today). Keep reading. Take the steps, no matter how dark or scary, no matter how many.

See you at the library!

Steps leading into the old library in Missouri Valley, Iowa

37

Holes!

I walked in the kitchen door. Mom's gaze immediately fell to my knees. Two jagged holes were framed by dirt-encrusted blue fabric. Twisted, ragged threads drooped sadly around each gash. Mother's pale-blue eyes quickly lifted to mine. "Are your knees scraped bad?"

At that moment the grazed, pink blotches of skin began to throb. I had spent the school day fretting about ruining my new, seam-up-the-middle, stretch pants. Not getting a scolding made me feel even worse. "Can you patch them?"

Mom shook her head. "I can patch them, but you won't be able to wear them to school."

I looked down, trying to hold back the tears. "Why not? I don't care if they have patches! I don't even care if they have holes." Though I was only seven at the time, I knew that last statement was not true. Without judgment, without criticism, without even spoken words that I remember, it was simply understood: Only kids from poor families wore clothes with obvious holes.

Yesterday my daughter walked in my kitchen. My gaze immediately fell to her jeans. Matching, jagged holes, in a diagonal waffle pattern gleamed from each leg, just above the knee. My brown eyes met her hazels. "Do you want me to patch those jeans?" She just laughed at the standing joke I made nearly every visit. Then I asked if I needed to buy her a new pair without holes in them. No matter how hard I try, I cannot shake my growing-up association with holes.

There were eight of us, and I'm sure we wore holes into hundreds of socks. I remember kneeling next to our mother's chair as she threaded her darning needle. Dad had worn a hole in the toe of his heavy wool socks. She reached for the light bulb tucked into the side of her sewing basket, slipped it into the top of the sock and pushed it carefully to the toe. An area of shiny glass appeared as the hole stretched to a neat little circle over the glass.

She threaded her darning needle with gray yarn, then patiently described the process while she worked. "You want to start stitching a ways from the hole." She wove the needle in and out until parallel threads lined the hole from top to bottom. "Then you weave the yarn through the other way." She started at the bottom of the hole and her needle flashed over, under, over, under the threads. Soon the hole was neatly filled in. None of the lightbulb showed.

I hurried upstairs and grabbed a pair of my worn-thin white cotton socks. There was a small hole on one toe.

Mom even let me use the lightbulb. I pushed it carefully, squeezing it through the sock until the bulb reached the toe and revealed the hole. I guided cotton thread into the eye of Mom's darning needle and began stitching a ways around the hole. I pushed the needle in at the top of the hole and pulled it out at the bottom. Lots of times. Then I ran the thread through those stitches the other way. Lots of times. At last, I felt the hole was well plastered with stitches aiming in every direction. With great ceremony, I snipped off the string and tied the beginning thread to the end thread in a giant knot.

I proudly showed Mom my work. She smiled a sort of crooked smile, but didn't say anything. The next day I pulled on my newly-darned socks. Soon my big toe complained of a sore spot right where the hole had been. Suddenly, I understood why Mom had not sung her usual praises.

Today, sixty-some years after my slightly over-zealous darning job, I discovered a hole in my white cotton sock. With great ceremony I strode to the rag drawer, pulled it open and deposited that sock right in the front.

Holes! No matter how hard I try, I cannot shake that association from my growing-up years.

38

How's that for Luck?

"Ma will have your hide if you slop all the milk out of that bucket!" Emma giggled at the extra spring in her older sister's step as they hurried to the house with the milk for the family. Their mother expected help with supper, and tonight the girls managed to leave the meanest cows, the ones that needed kickers, for their brothers to milk. The boys had teased their sister about being lucky; now she wouldn't end up an old maid. But Mabel just smiled. Nothing could affect her good spirits tonight.

Last night her beau had spoken to their father and asked for her hand. The couple met at a Swedish picnic back in July. Her sister, Ida, and her husband, Oscar, had invited Harrison. After a six month courtship, the young man asked Mabel to marry him. He had saved up and bought a piece of land with a house and a barn. With some luck and some rain, they would build a farm, a home, a life together.

Harrison was nervous as he sat across the table from Mabel's father. He spoke of his plans for the future and his hope to marry the man's daughter. Dad didn't appear very happy, but he finally agreed. "Ja, well, I suppose it's time she got married. Don't know what we'll do around here without her help. Probably have to sell off some of the milk cows."

Before the man could change his mind, Harrison stood and shook hands with his future father-in-law. Mabel followed her fiancé to the door and watched him climb into his flashy Ford Roadster. Peeking around her, Emma sighed dramatically and folded her hands over her heart. "I love his car!"

Since last night, Mabel dreamed of her husband-to-be, their future, their beautiful wedding. So, tonight, as she and Emma hustled up the snowy path, Mabel could no longer contain her excitement. "I am so happy! To think I am getting married!" (Emma sighed.) Mabel continued. "We must set a date. I think June would be nice. I will buy a new dress and maybe a pair of shoes." She thought of the money she had saved. Working for a neighbor, Mabel earned 75 cents a week. Keeping out only enough for a few clothes and Christmas gifts for her family, she managed to set aside a good sum for her future. Two years ago, she entrusted her father with her savings. He had agreed to keep it for her. Every week she gave him a bit more to add to it. She was so lucky she had thought to do this. Not only would she have money for a lovely wedding dress, she would have some to bring to their marriage. How wonderful if she could help purchase machinery, or maybe a batch of baby chicks...

She set her dreams aside as she and her sister stomped up the steps and into the porch. They left their wraps and rushed into the kitchen to set the table. Dad sat soberly, arms crossed in front of him. Ma stirred the corn in the kettle and mixed thickening for the gravy. A heavy silence loomed; a tension hung in the air as though strong words had been spoken, then interrupted. At last Ma spoke in Swedish, "It should be in March, before spring planting. Then there won't be time."

Mabel frowned. Were they discussing the wedding date? Shouldn't she have something to say about this?

Dad grunted. "Ja, well, get it done then."

Ma took down the wall calendar from Cargill Elevator and flipped to March. "It needs to be on a Wednesday. You know what they say, 'Monday for wealth, Tuesday for health, Wednesday the best day of all.' The 22nd should work if the preacher can come." Dad shrugged in resignation.

Mabel stopped short, plates in her hands. March 22 was less than three months away! She had so much to do to get ready for a wedding. She would help Ma clean the house; the wedding would be in the parlor. They needed to send invitations. She had to get her wedding dress. She would need money.

Mabel took a deep breath and turned to her father. "Dad, I will need my savings, all the money I have given you since I started working."

Moments of silence stretched to what seemed like hours. Finally, her father barked, "No."

Mom's parents, Selma and Adolf Anderson

39

How's that for Luck? Part II

"But..."

The cold look in her father's narrowed eyes defied any argument. No meant no. How could this be? How could a father withhold her own hard-earned money? How could he keep it when she needed it now for her wedding, for her future?

Mabel sat at supper in stunned silence. Emma stole sympathetic looks at her older sister as they washed and dried dishes. Mabel worked in rote, not allowing herself to think, not letting her heart feel the pain.

Finally, work finished, she lifted her chin and walked to the stairs and up to her room. She quietly closed the door behind her. Then she fell on her bed and let the tears of anguish flow. Why had she trusted her father to return her money? She had worked hard, always with hope that she was making a better future for herself and maybe someday, her husband. And to think she could not even buy a wedding dress! Why had she allowed herself to dream? Her body shook with sobs, engulfed in loss.

When no tears were left inside her, she blew her nose and slid off the bed. She strode to the small closet in the corner. Her best shoes were black and scufffed. No one would notice her feet anyway. Her Sunday dress was a gray and pink print. It would work.

"We're going to Watertown to buy you a wedding dress," Lilly announced the next day. "I'll help you," her sister said.

It was blue, and Mabel loved it. She dreamed of the perfect day as she sent the invitations. Julia and Ida helped scrub floors and wash curtains. She was lucky to have such good sisters.

The day before the wedding the groom was "sick as a dog," he said. But it was just the stomach flu, and nothing would keep him from their wedding.

March 22nd dawned brightly with only a few clouds. Mabel helped get the lunch ready. She and Emma got out the best dishes and silverware. Julia brought mints she had made and two giant cans of salted peanuts. Lilly brought the lovely white cake she had decorated with sky-blue roses.

That afternoon, with Lilly as the bridesmaid, Mabel and Harrison stood before the preacher in the parlor. Their parents, sisters, brothers, neighbors and friends surrounded them as "in sickness and health, for richer for poorer, for better for worse," they pledged their troth.

The crowd feasted on the wedding fare. The happy couple smiled through the teasing and the good wishes. The day was perfect.

Then it began to snow. Through the windows, they watched giant white flakes streak to the ground. Chairs scooted back, but by the time the men got to the door, the wind had picked up in typical South Dakota fashion. The report: "You can't see your hand in front of your face!"

The guests stayed. It was not safe to leave in such a blizzard, but surely it would let up soon and they could make their way home.

Around three in the morning, the wind died down. With promises to help each other get home, those who lived nearby left. The preacher declared that he was not going out in such weather. So the new bride and groom spent their wedding night at her home visiting with the preacher.

The next morning Mabel rushed upstairs to get her things. Quickly, she hugged her parents, invited them to come visit soon, and headed for the door—-before Dad told her to help with the milking.

They drove off in Harrison's eight-year-old Model A Ford to their piece of land with a house and a barn.

He showed her Bud and Riley in their stalls. He had sold the Roadster to get enough money to buy the old car AND a pair of horses.

He showed her their home. She clutched wedding treasures to her heart as she took in the kitchen furniture: one wooden chair and seven peach crates. It would work.

Days passed. The husband and wife worked side by side in the fields as the horses pulled the plow and the planter. Together they built their dream: a farm, a home and a life. Six children, sixteen grandchildren and more than fifty happy years together.

How's that for luck? No! How's that for love?

Our parents' wedding photo

40

With Heartfelt Gratitude

I just thought it was old, but obviously it was special to her. She smiled softly as her fingers wrapped around the single, curved brass handle on the tiger-oak frame and tugged the glass door open. Though I was only ten at the time, the next two hours of my life remain indelibly etched in my mind. For on that winter day, sitting next to our mother at the kitchen table, I learned the true meaning of gratitude.

"This was a wedding gift from my folks." Her blue eyes shone brightly as she reached for an oval glass tray with two "bowls" on it. Lovely pink and red roses were painted on the front of each. "It's for cream and sugar," Mom explained to me as she reverently placed the set on the table and wiped the dust from the tops.

I decided they must have needed a lot of those cream and sugar things back in the day because she brought out another pair, these of shiny glass, textured in what looked like dents. It was also a wedding gift, from the neighbors, and she spoke their names.

At the back of the cabinet was an iridescent vase with a gold rim. "Julia gave me this for my birthday a long time ago." I wondered if my aunt knew then how much her sister would love her flowers.

A round ceramic teapot came out next, spotted with bright red, green and blue polka dots. I knew this was a gift from Lilly, another of her sisters. Sometimes Mom would get it out and make tea, just for the two of us.

She loved every treasure in that old wooden hutch and the person who gave it to her.

Was Mom grateful because at times in her life she had so little? Was it because she grew up with very few gifts?

Whatever the reason, I cannot help but think that her grateful attitude affected how she and Dad raised their children. From a very young age we were taught to say "thank you."

Many times at that same kitchen table Mom sat by each of us as we penciled words onto cards. When we received gifts, we wrote thank yous. A dollar bill tucked into a birthday card? We wrote a note. Though our parents probably never heard of Emily Post and her books of proper etiquette, they made it clear that we all needed to show our appreciation and do it right. We couldn't get by with "thanks for the present." Oh, no! What we wrote was just as important as THAT we wrote. It was critical that we showed the giver how much we appreciated their gift.

Looking back at all those times spent at the kitchen table, I have a feeling Mom was teaching us more than how to say "thank you." By the way she lived, the way she treasured all the gifts in her life, she experienced the joy of being truly grateful. I think that in her heart she wanted us to feel it, too.

The old china cabinet

A "cream and sugar" set, one of our parents' wedding gifts

41

And Now—A Word From Our Sponsor

Nearly every night of my growing-up years, at least some of the family spent our last waking hours in front of our 15-inch black and white Zenith. Sponsors paid to air the shows, so commercials engaged about nine minutes of every hour of TV time. It was the golden age of television advertising, and occasionally we found the ads as entertaining as the programs.

Though we were often glued to the set, we were totally immune to the ad messages. At a very young age, we were taught that "they just want us to buy stuff we don't need." So, even though we stared at the screen, mouth agape, we knew we were above the producer's popular powers of persuasion. No sirree, Bob! We would not fall for some company telling us we had to buy their stuff.

Dinah Shore, who produced the commercials for her own show, encouraged Americans to "see the USA in their Chevrolet." Our parents did some traveling about the country, but Dad was a Ford man.

Mom sniffed in disdain when the Wisk parrot cried "Ring around the collar!" humiliating the poor housewife as she examined her husband's stained white shirt. Our mother used Tide. She claimed Tide cleaned up collars just fine, but you can bet she paid close attention to those shirt collars as she pressed the iron over them. No parrot was going to screech over her shoulder.

The "Little Dab'll do ya" Brylcreem tube had a spot in our mirrored cabinet. Probably there were no other hair gel products on the grocery shelf when Don or Delmer needed it. The ad slogan, "Keeps hair looking clean and natural" never entered their minds. Certainly not!

My sisters preferred Doublemint gum. They chose to spend their nickels on the green package because they liked it best. They were certainly NOT influenced by the harmonious hype of the Doublemint Twins, "Double your pleasure, double your fun!"

The pleasant scent of Dial soap wafted from the bathroom soap dish. Practicality prevailed; we used Dial because it got us clean. NEVER did the thought enter our minds that if we used a different bar, we might smell offensive to others: "Aren't you glad you use Dial? Don't you wish everybody did?"

I never did figure out what the "something" was about an Aqua Velva man, but I do remember when Dad splashed it on I decided that he probably didn't need Dial soap for the rest of the week.

As the youngest and most rebellious of the family, I sometimes stood before the bathroom sink mirror checking for yellow as I brushed my teeth (with Crest) and sang, "You'll wonder where your teeth all went when you brush your teeth with Pepsodent."

Meat manufacturers pushed hot dogs and targeted children with jaunty jingles like "Hot dogs, Armour hot dogs, what kind of kids eat Armour hot dogs?" Oscar Mayer added a taste of humor in its ad with singing rivals. The little pony-tailed girl leads the group with "Oh I'd love to be an Oscar Mayer wiener; that is what I'd really like to be-e-e, cuz if I were an Oscar Mayer wiener, everyone would be in love with me." The little boy counters, "Oh, I'm glad I'm not an Oscar Mayer wiener..." (I sided with the boy.)

Likely, you were immune to those television commercials, too, and just tuned them out like we did.

You probably don't remember the choruses of children and adults, the provocative female voices, or the orchestras and bold brass bands where lyrics and melody joined forces: "Plop, plop, fizz fizz, oh what a relief it is." "Things go better with Coke." "My dog's better than your dog, my dog's better than yours..." "You can trust your car to the man who wears the star..." "Mr. Clean gets rid of dirt and grime and everything that's in it..." "Nothing says lovin' like something from the oven and Pillsbury says it best!"

So, how long will it take to stop singing them in your head?

42

The Other Side of the Furrow

Thursday morning as I crossed the Boyer River Bridge, a flock of birds approached my car, flitting and darting like children playing tag. They circled directly above and I could see their snow-white undersides and outstretched wings. A darker area circled their heads and beaks. Seagulls! My mind flew back to a long-ago stubble field just up the road from our house. I sat in the fence row and waited for Dad to finish the round with his John Deere tractor.

The shiny steel blades of the moldboard plow turned the earth over into a black, bumpy furrow. Behind the plow hundreds of white birds landed and lifted and circled back to repeat the process. From a distance they looked like small strips of ribbon fluttering in the breeze. My seven-year-old brain decided those creatures were the coolest ever. I wondered if they were ours. Did Jensens and Pages have their own plow assistants? How did they know when to swoop in? Did they have a gull scout?

My sisters also clearly remember the birds in the field on those cool South Dakota afternoons. The distinct earthy smell that permeated the air nestles in Deloris' and Darlene's memories. Dorothy recalls the cheerful cries the birds made as they gracefully glided above the furrow. Dad told her the birds were seagulls as the two sat in the yellow curve of the tractor tire, enjoying lunch. All-in-all, pleasant pictures prevail as we look back at those delightful birds that homed in our memory banks.

The "Delmer Laugh" sounded through my speaker phone when I mentioned the birds to my brother. I had a feeling I was going to get a different perspective and he didn't disappoint. He described their feeding frenzy as each descended to the dirt, grabbed a worm, tipped up its head and swallowed it in split second time. Then it flew around a few seconds, waiting for the next chance. "They got a little close for comfort, even as I was sitting up on the tractor. Occasionally huge splats of white hit the hood of the 730." I could hear a smile in my brother's voice. "Yeah, I used to look around at all those birds and wonder how many I could get in one shot with the 12-guage."

A sense of fondness filled his next laugh as he described our older brother's experience with the seagulls. "Fowl" described the birds well in Don's opinion. There were hundreds of them hovering around on one particular fall day. (Maybe the neighbors were not using theirs.) They kept flying around the tractor and overhead, screeching at him. He decided it would be best not to look up. Sure enough, liquid bombs started hitting the tractor, then the steering wheel. It was the last straw when he felt a huge plop on the brim of his cap. Smelly white splatters suddenly coated the tractor panel.

At quitting time Don hurtled into the yard and pulled the plow into the Quonset. He strode purposefully to the cattle tank and swished his cap through the water. With a look of pure disgust, he handed the cap to Mom. She stared at it for a few seconds. Finally, she looked at her young son—-and laughed!

It is true that each of us remembers things differently. As in life, our perspective depends on our experiences. It all depends on whether we are riding in front of the furrow or watching the world from behind it.

The next time a flock of gulls flies over me, I will fondly recall the seabirds as I watched from the end of the field. But, a new picture now nests in the nooks and crannies of my mind—a picture of Don and his polka dotted cap. Thank you, my brothers, for adding smiles to my memories!

Author's note: Since I live less than 15 miles from the DeSoto National Wildlife Refuge, I emailed Peter Rea, the Supervisory Park Ranger there. He said they have been seeing a lot of gulls on the refuge, especially the ring-billed gulls. He offered a website and profile. At the end of the article there is a black and white photo of the birds. They are following a plow.

43

When Life Gives Us Wind

For two days the north wind has howled through the trees and rammed into windows here in southwest Iowa. Fifty-five miles-per-hour gales put us in a wind advisory area more times than I care to remember. I have asked locals if we are having more wind than usual. They say yes, there is more wind, a lot more than normal.

If you ask people what memories they have of wind, unfortunately, most involve destruction and loss.

My brother Delmer remembers a year when the weather challenged even the toughest farmers. It started out as a normal year. Winter snows left moisture in the earth with promise of spring growth and hopes for a good crop. When the oak leaves were the size of a squirrel's ear Dad said it was time to plant so he attached the four-row planter to the John Deere 520 and headed to the 40-acre field south of the house. He wire-checked corn back then, so every time he reached the fence row he climbed down and moved the knotted wire that stretched the length of the field. Yellow wheels turned and the wire knots clicked as the planter dropped four golden kernels in the precise spot in each row. It was tedious work, but our father and his sons took great pride in their checked rows that would allow cultivating in any direction.

In less than a week tiny green shoots pushed through the warm soil and pointy ribbons of green stood in formation as they reached for the South Dakota sun. But some years Mother Nature moves in and wrenches our hopes away. One May night temperatures fell far below freezing. The next day, bright green corn seedlings morphed to dull brown and bent sadly to the soil in the morning sun.

"Some of it will grow back," Dad said as we drove by the field, "if we get some rain." But rainfall was far below normal that year. Hopeful white roots reached down, desperately searching for moisture that was not there. Leaves could not grow without water. The plants waited while the black earth that nurtured them baked to light gray and mutated to a flimsy dust.

One June morning, a gust of wind fluttered the weakened leaves. Another stronger rush followed. Soon savage gales of 50 miles per hour clawed at the soil. As happened in the drought of the Dirty Thirties, it picked up the dry dust and hurled it into the air. Sharp as a razor, the whirling particles pelted the corn plants and cut them to the ground.

That evening Dad, Don and Delmer took the pickup for a drive around the section. They surveyed the wind's devastation in their precious corn fields. Hill tops and northern exposures lay stripped, as bare as if nothing had been planted there. Hardly ten plants survived the wicked teeth of the dust-laden tempest. Sparse green plants held on in the low lying areas and on the southern hillsides.

We ended up cutting the corn for silage that year. Dad took the opportunity to point out why it was important to raise other crops as well as livestock. "You don't put all your eggs in one basket." With the eternal hope of a farmer he added, "Next year will be better. Maybe it will be a normal year."

Though spring, 2022 has barely settled in, many in our country have already experienced the wind's horrible destruction. Though they will always remember the devastation and loss, we pray for them, that they will have the strength to go on.

And the hope that next year will be better...

44

We Can't Stop the Music!

There are hundreds, maybe thousands of them lying dormant in our brains, just waiting. Suddenly, at any given time, a signal triggers a part of our memories, and uninhibited, spontaneous song pours out. Whether we belt the songs out loud or they play silently again and again in our heads, we can't stop the music.

About once a month I stop in to see a dear couple in Missouri Valley. Sometime during the course of our visit, the husband heads downstairs, and within a few minutes glorious vibrato chords rise up to us from the electric organ. Presto! The music memories unfold and the lyrics dance about in our heads. His wife and I name the songs: "Red Roses for a Blue Lady," Let Me Call You Sweetheart," "Side by Side," "Moon River." We remember. We smile.

A group of Dartmouth researchers has learned that the brain's auditory cortex, the part that handles information from our ears, holds on to musical memories. The phenomenon is called involuntary musical imagery.

I can't help but wonder how some of those musical images keyed into my brain. As a kid, I was a rock and roll fan. Old, gushy love songs were not cool for my generation. I remember Saturday nights when trumpets blared the theme music for one of my favorite TV shows, "Get Smart." I plopped down, anticipating the antics of inept spy Maxwell Smart (Don Adams) and Agent 99 (Barbara Feldon.) Just as Max injured his nose on the last door into CONTROL

Headquarters in the opening credits, Dad glanced at his watch. "DeAnn, turn the channel. Lawrence Welk is on." With a huge sigh, and a groan (a quiet groan), I got up and switched stations. (I was the remote back then.) To show my disdain, I stomped to the kitchen and read a book. Did the wunnerful-wunnerful songs crooned by Norma Zimmer soak into my brain in spite of me not wanting to listen?

Likely, the stored up memories originate from many sources: television, church, music class, radio, concerts, and baseball games. Sisters singing around the piano, "Bless This House." Delmer and Neil strumming guitars and singing in the living room, "My Baby Does the Hanky Panky" and "The House of the Rising Sun."

Just as we don't know when or what melodies were melded into our auditory cortexes, we never know what will trip the switch that releases the music memories.

I asked each of my siblings what song stuck in their head and was most likely to pour out at any reminder. Delmer's is "Amarillo, by Morning." The Beatles' classic, "Hard Day's Night" is Darlene's most-likely recalled song.

"The Little Brown Church in the Vale" is the song most dear to the childhood of my sister, Deloris. Her adept fingers on the keys of the old upright piano brought the song to life many times in our living room.

Dorothy obviously loved music class, as she thought of "Kookaburra Sits in the Old Gum Tree." "Over the River and Through the Woods" can easily kick in. The melody helped their family pass the miles on long drives to Grandmother's house.

The fascinating thing is that we don't even have to actually hear the song. A word or two from the title or lyrics can bring out the music in us. Sometimes the songs won't stop playing, but often they are fun to remember. The backup singers sway to the music. Can you see Ricky Nelson's gorgeous blue eyes as he sang "Hello Mary Lou?"

Have any of these songs flowed from your auditory cortex? Once they start, you can't stop them. I cannot help but imagine the same songs dancing through the heads of thousands of newspaper readers across the country. Just in case none of these tripped the trigger in your brain, try to resist this one: "We All Live in a Yellow Submarine, Yellow Submarine, Yellow Submarine…"

I'm smiling.

45

Now that's Entertainment!

The man in front of me in the checkout lane examined the contents of his wallet and shook his head. He glanced up at his cohort, another guy about his age. "I may have to get another job if Paul (name changed to protect the innocent) keeps asking for money. Twice now he wanted $70 to take his girlfriend to some fancy restaurant in Omaha."

The gentleman next to him chuckled. "Don't feel bad. Every weekend my kid asks for money to go out with friends. I don't even know if they talk while they're eating. I think they stare at their phones the whole time! It's not like when we were young."

My unintentional eavesdropping ushered in thoughts of the years when my siblings and I grew up in rural South Dakota. Farm life offered plenty of opportunities for things to do. (We definitely knew better than to mention the word "bored.") As we reached the teen years, we wanted to hang out with friends. In typical teenage tradition, we longed to fit in, but being cool allowed different activities back then.

Nearly every summer weekend, a ride to a nearby town (average gas price was 31 cents per gallon) and a dollar to cover admission and snacks provided an evening of excitement. Baseball! From the sound system in the crow's nest the announcer gave spectators a powerful play-by-play of the game. Car horns blared at amazing outfield catches and ninth inning grand slams. Our cheers carried on far longer when the super star happened to be our brother or friend.

The smooth cement floor of the De Smet Armory invited wheels—roller wheels. For a fifty cent (or less) admission and a quarter for skate rental, skaters of all ages circled the rink to music. If a cute boy (it was the boy's job to do the asking) asked me to skate, I declared silently that I would never wash my sweaty hand again and began looking forward to next week's skating time.

During December the Ritz Theater in De Smet offered free Saturday matinees for youngsters. Every year Delmer and I took in at least one. Gene Autry starred in a classic Western, "Valley of Fire." Captain Sinbad saved a dangling damsel in distress several times in his "Seventh Journey." It seemed to me that we saw the same old movies year after year, but we never turned down the chance to go.

The theater also provided entertainment for weekend nights. Dad told Delmer and me to have a good time as he handed us each a couple dollars for the movie. The enticing aroma of buttery popcorn followed us to our fold-down seats. Sometimes we bought popcorn or Milk Duds. Though Dad never ordered us to bring back the change, we did. I clearly remember coming home from a movie and proudly depositing leftover change into Dad's hand. He chuckled softly and handed it back. "You go put that in your piggy bank."

Dorothy and her friends viewed the latest Elvis movies *Viva Las Vegas* and *Beach Blanket Bingo* on the silver screen. Mom and Dad took me to see *The Sound of Music*, which was highly recommended by my piano teacher.

Teen Town was a popular hangout in De Smet for a few years. Delmer recalls listening to big name Rock and Roll bands at the youth center. The Cavaliers, a group from the Arlington and Lake Preston area, and Myron Lee and the Caddies performed at Teen Town on their way to fame.

The entertainment we chose didn't cost a lot back then. Sometimes it was free. On warm Sunday afternoons my sisters challenged peers to a friendly battle of croquet on the front lawn. The good-natured banter through the game likely turned to triumphant teasing, for almost always, the girls won. On Friday evenings friends gathered around the kitchen table for a few rounds of ping pong. Some games got rather intense. The longer the ball stayed in play, the louder the hoots of triumph and the groans of defeat. The losing player immediately demanded a consolation game.

Always there was fun. Always there was laughter. Decades later, we remember. Now THAT'S entertainment!

46

Just Hit the High Spots

"The preacher's coming!" Dad announced to Mom as he placed the old black phone back on its cradle. Mom quickly took in the "lived-in" look of our farmhouse and rushed to remove the pile of mail from the table. (After all, cleanliness is next to godliness!)

"Quick! Hit the high spots!" We knew what she meant; we had only a few minutes to get the place looking acceptable for company. The boys grabbed their school books and carried them to their bedroom. Deloris filled the kitchen sink with hot soapy water and soon, with Darlene drying, they had every dirty dish clean, dried and back in the cupboard. Dorothy grabbed the dust rag and she and I headed for the living room. She dusted around the lamps and photos. Just as I straightened the Bible on its doily on the bottom book shelf, we heard the knock on the door.

Months later another phone call foretold the arrival of more guests—-the uncle and his family from the east. "We're going through South Dakota and wanted to stop and see you folks." They would arrive in the morning.

Mom kept the place pretty clean all the time, but company called for extra measures. Since we only had a few hours, she instructed, "Give it a lick and a promise." That meant to do the best we could for now and later we would do a more thorough job. We picked up our rooms, cleared dresser tops and used the dust mop to sweep out dust bunnies from under the beds. (Mom didn't think it was funny when I told her I was growing mine to jackrabbit size.) We swept and mopped all floors and vacuumed the rugs. (We called them rugs, not carpets.) One of the girls wiped fingerprints from the white metal cabinets.

The next morning a bouquet of fresh flowers on the kitchen table and a pretty clean house greeted the relatives.

The occasional spiff-up for company and the weekly maintenance kept the house in good shape, but when April came and Mom caught the spring cleaning bug, we took "clean" to a whole new level. "We've got to use some elbow grease," Mom told us.

Every floor was swept and scrubbed. Vacuums sucked up dirt in corners and edges. A rag tied to the broom worked to sweep down cobwebs.

Our mother took pride in her kitchen and each spring every surface in that room, ceiling to floor, was scrubbed, polished or dusted. We took down curtains and shades and washed the windows. Mom had to give her stamp of approval before they could be pushed back in place. "Did you get the corners? We don't want any streaks." Soon freshly laundered, starched and ironed curtains fluttered in the breeze.

Years flew by. Technology advanced faster than during any time in history. Suddenly we could do more, travel faster and stay in touch with more people than ever. Priorities shifted. Comedian Phyllis Diller touted her house cleaning philosophy to the world: "Housework can't kill you, but why take a chance?"

Today, if my pastor called to say she is coming, I would take a look at my "lived-in" house. Would I quickly hit the high spots? Well, maybe the tallest mountain peaks. Much more importantly, I would start the coffee pot.

Company coming from a distance? I might need to clear a path through the spare bedroom where I have deposited all the projects I plan to work on later.

Spring cleaning? So far I have swept down cobwebs from the ceiling and washed two windows.

Likely, I will accomplish a few more things, but in the meantime, it is imperative to get things into proper perspective. What is truly important in life? And, what exactly, are the high spots?

47

Reflections on the Kitchen Table

A shiny chrome edge surrounded the gray-swirled Formica top. Four tubular legs curved out slightly, then turned down to the floor. Chairs matched, sporting vinyl seats and backs and more shiny legs. The fashion at the time, this table replaced the massive oak table shortly after I was born.

As newborns, Mom laid us on a thick towel on the table and gave us our first baths in the kitchen, warmed by the woodstove in the corner. She gently rubbed the washcloth under our chins and behind our ears. My sisters remember her smiling and humming softly as her baby happily flailed arms and legs.

We grew older and the table served as the family gathering place. Mealtime meant conversation as well as bountiful food. The whole family kept tabs on corn planting progress and the condition of Tiny, the new calf. Friday night's game would require early chores. No need to write down events (no cell phones on which to enter them), supper time communication kept us organized.

When I was four, I followed Mom wherever she went, always wanting to help. "You can clean the table," she said one day, pulling out rags from a drawer. "Get it all shined up." I was just polishing the grooved edge when Dad came in. He bent down and whistled.

"That's so shiny you can almost see yourself!" I beamed with pride—and rubbed harder!

At the table we learned patience and gratitude. We may have been itching to get outside to the swing or playhouse or sandbox, but we sat while our father finished dessert and lingered over his coffee. After a meal no one left until Dad stood and thanked Mom, often with a kiss on the cheek.

Dorothy remembers one Father's Day when each of us bought or made a small gift and set it at Dad's place. He sat and looked at the stack for a few seconds before he opened and smiled at each one. Tears filled his eyes as he regarded his family gathered around him at that kitchen table.

Some winter evenings the whole crew gathered for a game of Monopoly or Yahtzee. Math skills, strategy and sportsmanship emanated from sessions at the table. Occasionally, Sunday dinner meant a sermon after the sermon.

The table was a place to learn by watching and doing. Mom rolled pie crusts and kneaded bread. Our first attempts were far from perfect. "That is how we learn," Mom said. And we did.

Saturdays meant butchering chickens. I recall the not-very-pleasant smell as Mom worked at the table, cutting and cleaning the birds, but I never turned down fried chicken for Sunday dinner!

Scales flew up and stuck on my face as I stood next to the table and rubbed the scaler over the small perch. Following a successful fishing trip, we all had a part in getting the fish ready for the frypan and freezer.

Company came. "Pull up a chair!" Dad invited and Mom put the coffee on. Neighbors, aunts and uncles dropped in to share news. Stories, memories and laughter made history at our kitchen table.

Decorated cakes and ham sandwiches adorned the lace-covered table at confirmation and graduation parties. The honoree stood by and greeted our guests.

The table held us up in sad times, too. I watched from a corner as Mom and her three remaining sisters sat in our kitchen, heads bowed, and arms leaning on the Formica surface. Tears fell as they remembered the good times with their beloved sister, Lily, whom they lost much too soon.

The old kitchen table was the place for learning and growing, for laughter and tears. It was the center of love. Look back at your kitchen table, the one from your growing-up years. Maybe, just maybe you will see your own reflection—-the reflection of your life.

Delmer and I doing homework at the old kitchen table

48

The Story of the 13th Little Pig—-Part 1

"Dad, come quick! The sow's having her pigs!" The screen door slammed shut as Delmer rushed back out to the hog house. Dad reached for his jacket on the hook behind the door. The guys had been watching the old Landrace, knowing she was due to farrow any time.

"Can I come watch?" Dad glanced at Mom for her approval. She didn't say no, but she didn't look too happy, either. She knew how heartbreaking animal births could be when things didn't go right. I grabbed my sweatshirt and raced to catch up with Dad's long strides.

Delmer peered through the wooden boards at the long white sow lying in the straw. Dad stood behind him for a few seconds. "She's got twelve," Delmer whispered. "But she stopped." He glanced back at Dad with the question in his eyes. Was something wrong?

My hands grasped the bottom board as I knelt next to the pen. I watched the piglets nose around their mama on unsteady legs. Their soft, high-pitched squeaks blended with their mother's breathy grunts. Time seemed to stand still as we waited. Was the sow growing weaker? Why was nothing happening? "Sometimes it takes a while." Dad must have read my thoughts.

Finally, after what seemed like forever to a five-year-old, the sow's short curly tail circled and another tiny piglet entered the world. This one did not move. We waited and watched. At last, Dad crawled into the pen. He reached down to the newborn and rubbed his hand over its side. "He's breathing, but he doesn't look good." He lifted the tiny piglet up and made sure his nose was clear. "Come on, little guy! Let's get you something to eat." Dad moved to the mother's side, found an open dispenser at the milk bar and nuzzled the small pink nose against the mother pig. There was no response; the nearly-lifeless form rested limply against Dad's hand. "I don't think he's gonna make it."

Sadness shone in our father's eyes as I stared up at him. "Dad, can I try to save him?"

He shook his head, almost certain that if he said yes, his little girl's heart would be broken. Big brown puppy eyes pleaded up at him. At last he relented. "Keep him warm. Mom will know what to do." He helped me tuck the little body inside my sweatshirt and I hurried up to the house.

Mom's eyes were sad, too, when I unwrapped the baby. "He probably won't make it," she warned me as she went to get a small box from the porch and set it on a chair next to the stove. "Get some rags and cover him up."

I knelt next to the box, rubbing the small white head with my fingers. Tears trickled down my face. "Come on, guy, you've GOT to make it!"

Mom warmed some top milk in a small pan on the woodstove. She added an egg and a few drops of Karo syrup and whipped it with a fork, testing the temperature with her finger. When she was satisfied that the mix was just right, she found a small spoon and knelt next to me. "We'll try and get something in his tummy." She held the little rag-wrapped bundle up and opened his mouth while I spooned in a few drops. She gently rubbed a finger down his throat to get him to swallow. Again and again we tried, as rivulets trickled out his mouth and down his sides. Finally, we cleaned off the spilled formula and tucked him back into his warm box. I kept constant vigil. Every hour I tried to get him to swallow a few drops.

That night before bed Dad put his hand on my shoulder and gazed down at the still form. "Sometimes we lose them. It's part of nature. Part of farming. You did your best. You get to bed now."

"He's still breathing. I'm going to get up in the night and feed him." Dad managed a sad smile and headed upstairs. I reached in and petted the little pig's head one last time. With a fervent prayer in my heart, I covered the box with a towel and trudged up to bed. *To be continued...*

49

The Story of the 13th Little Pig—-Part 2

I was mad at myself when I woke up because I knew I had slept more than an hour and Mom told me the baby pig needed to eat real often. He was the last of the litter and dreadfully weak. Dad and Mom both warned me that he probably wouldn't make it, but I was determined to try and save him. I was expecting the worst when I rushed down the steps and into the kitchen.

Wait! What was that noise? A faint scratching sound was coming from the box next to the stove! My heart pounded as I reached for the light switch. I pulled back the towel that covered the cardboard box. The little piglet's head wobbled and his front feet moved just slightly. As fast as I could, I warmed some of the "formula" Mom had made. This time he opened his mouth and tried sucking on the spoon. His tiny teeth clicked on the metal and a bit of liquid went down his throat.

The next morning soft baby-pig grunts sounded from the box. After two days and many messy feedings, the piglet was on his feet. I named him Snooper. We found a bigger box.

Nights grew warm and the little pig became more active, so the folks decided he could move outside. His home was an old doghouse in the corner of the yard. The second I stepped outside, Snooper would squeal happily and gallop out to see me. Like an adoring puppy, he followed me everywhere. If I sat in the grass, the little pig would plop next to me, contentedly waiting for a behind-the-ear scratch. Every day for weeks, we both basked in the South

Dakota sun.

Snooper learned to drink his milk from a bowl. His flat button snout rooted through the liquid making loud slurping sounds. In less than ten seconds, the bowl was clean and he looked up for more. Soon he learned to chomp down pig starter pellets. Snooper grew.

Pigs are naturally curious animals. They are constantly sticking their noses in something. One day Snooper decided to investigate the laundry hanging on the clothesline. He stretched his nose up high, but the only thing he could reach was Mom's flannel nightgown. At first he just sniffed it, obviously enjoying the fresh Tide scent. Then he opened his mouth and tugged at the bottom. The gown dropped over his head and Snooper panicked. For a few seconds a rose print nightgown tore through the yard like a ghost, arms flailing wildly to the ground on each side.

It was not long after that when Dad said Snooper needed to go to the pasture with the other young pigs. Sadly, I left the front yard, my porcine shadow following right behind me. I opened the pasture gate. Snooper stopped and sniffed the air. He stared for a few seconds at his siblings cavorting about in the pasture. Finally, he looked up at me, gave a happy grunt and hightailed out to join them, curly tail wiggling in the air.

That summer I often walked to the hog pasture to check on my small friend. At first he came to the fence and let me scratch behind his ears, but eventually he just looked up at me and went on with his grazing and playing. Time passed. Snooper grew up and went in the way of most farm animals. But I will never forget that little miracle pig, the 13th little pig—- the one that everyone said probably wouldn't make it.

50

Who's the Birdbrain?

We live in the information age. One can ask a question by speaking into a phone or entering a few key strokes. Within seconds, a plethora of particulars flashes across the screen. Sometimes the information is trustworthy, but sometimes...

Back in March a bewildered birdwatcher posted a question on a popular social media site: Why do birds peck at my window? Experts immediately twittered back the answer. When birds peck at your window they are seeing their reflection and think it is another bird. They are defending their territory.

At the time cardinals, finches, chickadees and woodpeckers visited the feeders outside my living room window. At least once every morning someone crashed into the glass. Clunk! Concussions were common, but none of them EVER pecked at my window.

Until one day, happy as larks, two new couples fluttered into the neighborhood: rose-breasted grosbeaks. The colorful males with red and white bandanas on their throats and the black and white striped females visited the feeders frequently. Unlike the other birds, the grosbeaks did not frantically fly when they saw movement on my side of the window. If I reached for my coffee or scratched my nose, the finches and cardinals flew the coop. Not the grosbeaks. They remained on the feeders and stared at me through the window. Obviously, from their bird's-eye view, I was not a threat. I looked forward to morning coffee watching the colorful critters.

Then, the dreaded "bird flu" swooped in, threatening the life of every winged wonder. Federal agencies warned bird lovers that feeding songbirds could spread the disease. They recommended pulling all feeders until spring migration ended, especially if you had a backyard chicken flock.

Reluctantly, I took down the feeders. Morning coffee would not be the same. The birds immediately missed their breakfast bar. For a few days, cardinals and finches perched in the trees, searching for the cafeteria. Eventually, they stopped coming around, except for four particular red, white and black creatures. The rose-breasted grosbeaks returned day after day. They watched from the bare branches of the burning bush. They settled on the empty wire hangers. They glared at me through my living room window.

Then it happened. The larger of the two males approached the glass. He flew in place as I watched, only two feet away. He pecked at the window! Within seconds, the other male followed suit. These were angry birds, fearlessly communicating their complaint: "Hey, lady! We need food!" For weeks, the four persisted. Beaks bopped. My morning coffee changed from sweet song to first week percussion practice.

The literary device for giving animals human characteristics is called anthropomorphism. Was I giving the creatures more credit than they deserved? Did these birds, with brains the size of a hazelnut, actually have the mental capacity to hold me responsible for sudden menu adjustments?

I considered the opinion of the experts. Was it possible that the grosbeaks were simply pecking at their reflections, thinking they were battling the competition? Maybe I was giving them human attributes and only imagining their vengeful behavior.

I looked out the window. As if reading my thoughts, the bird with the bigger bandanna flew up to my window. He glared in at me. No clunks, no pecking at the glass. But as he flew off, I noticed something on my window. There, directly in the center, was a round white splotch. In horrified realization, I watched the liquid dribble down the glass!

Eventually, I put the feeders up again. The cardinals, finches and woodpeckers are back. The grosbeaks bring new meaning to the phrase "eating like a bird." Again I enjoy my morning coffee, complete with the antics of my feathered friends.

No one pecks at the window. No more white, oozy splats adorn the glass. I am glad the grosbeaks are back on good behavior. But sometimes I cannot help but wonder—-just who is the birdbrain here?

<h1 style="text-align:center">51</h1>

<h1 style="text-align:center">Growing Up Under the Stars</h1>

An afternoon rain shower put an end to field work one warm day in early June. Delmer and the neighbor boys grabbed the opportunity to patrol the shelter belt for deer trails and broods of young pheasants. Not yet 10, the three enjoyed their frequent treks through the trees on the farm.

At the edge of the woods they crawled up on a five-foot boulder and sat, surveying the woods around them. "Hey, we should camp out down here. That would be so cool!" Delmer jumped down and pulled a dead branch away from the rock. The others joined in and soon cleared a perfect place for a campsite.

The next night the little red wagon bounced over the path through the trees. Three boys took turns pulling and walking alongside the wagon to keep the contents from toppling. A big paper sack filled with their mothers' food offerings hovered on top of three army blankets and the big green tarp. Excited about their first night under the stars, they reached the big rock in record time. All that work getting to the campsite made them hungry, so they decided to eat first, celebrating their first taste of independence with cookies and Kool Aid.

Rod scanned the lower tree branches. "We can hang the tarp over that one." Darkness settled in as they unfolded the heavy canvas and tried tossing it over the branch. Randy was about to crawl up the tree when a volley of thunder rumbled in the west. Lightning flashed. Shadows fluttered eerily as the tree

144

tops bent in the wind.

With the loaded wagon jostling behind them, the youngsters made it back to the front yard just as the storm let loose.

A year later, the boys ventured back to the woods for another overnight adventure. They set up the makeshift tent. Grommets on the edges of the tarp allowed them to tie the edges together. Though wide gaps remained, they were proud of their handiwork.

"At least there won't be a storm tonight." Randy gazed at the round moon, peeking through the leaves.

"Yeah, nothing's gonna make us go home. We'll make it all night this time." Delmer helped himself to another bologna sandwich. Stories and laughter blended with the night sounds of the forest. The air grew damp and cold. Warm blankets beckoned from their tent and soon sleep won.

Suddenly Delmer jerked awake. A pungent odor hovered in the air, over-powering his senses. "Hey, you guys, wake up! There must be a skunk out there!" The three struggled to tie the openings more securely, but holes still gaped at the bottom.

Visions of being trapped in a tent with a wild-tailed skunk danced through their heads. "Let's run home," Delmer voiced their common consensus. "The tent and stuff will be OK until morning."

The next year Delmer drove the pickup to the approach south of the grove, a different place to camp. Here the cottonwood and ash stood taller, older. There were open spaces where dead trees had fallen.

Three near-teens carried a tarp, blankets, cooler, a wire grate, Mom's cast iron skillet, and tools from under the pickup seat. Soon the tarp was draped over a branch. Strong wire fastened the openings shut at both ends.

They gathered branches and short logs and soon flames flickered in the darkness. Wood popped and tiny sparks flew as the fire warmed the night. When they got hungry, they pounded wood stakes around the fire to hold the grate. As flames subsided, the campers cooked supper. Hamburger sizzled in the frypan. When it was browned, they added two cans of pork and beans. Someone chanted "Beans, beans, the musical fruit..." Another glanced at the tarp and suggested that they might want to undo the wire closings.

The boys agreed that their cooking was the best they ever tasted. What was left of supper remained in the frypan on the grate as they talked into the wee hours of the morning. Embers still glowed as they sighed happily and crept into their shelter.

At the first streak of dawn, three tired campers emerged. They stopped short at the sight before them. The campsite had been trashed! Stakes leaned. The grate protruded from the ashes. A perfectly clean skillet sat just in front of the tent. Probable culprits flashed through each young man's mind.

Three years. Three boys. They grew and matured, prepared to take on the next stage of their lives with a growing sense of independence. It all began as a tiny spark, fanned and nurtured under the South Dakota stars.

<h1 style="text-align:center">52</h1>

Something We Can Count On

It's always good to know there are things in life we can count on. Flip a switch and let there be light. Turn a faucet and Voila! Water pours forth! Every morning just before dawn I can count on a wake-up call from Brooster. Actually 20 wake-up calls—at least.

Brooster is my Delaware-Cuckoo Maran-cross rooster. He is NOT a sweet, lovable cuddly critter. Once a week, Brooster sneaks up behind me (obviously thinking he needs to assert himself as the alpha male), ready to attack. His two-inch spurs have connected with my legs several times. I once promised myself I would never keep a mean rooster, but two factors have prevented Brooster from becoming chicken noodle: First of all, a rooster ensures fertile eggs in the event that I want to hatch chicks. Secondly, I count on Brooster to defend the flock. Weasels, hawks, bobcats, coyotes and other predators abound here in the country. I have read that roosters will fight to the death for their women. Every morning when I hear that rooster crow, I smile and go back to sleep, secure in the knowledge that my chickens have a protector.

But this morning something was different. First-light song birds broke the morning silence, calling and answering through the trees. I waited for Brooster. No cock-a-doodle-do. No daily wake-up calls. Nothing.

Images of the dreaded weasel flew into my head. Had one slipped through wires? Were Brooster and all the hens lying dead in bloody carnage? I pictured poor Brooster, dying a hero's death.

I stepped into my chicken-print Sloggers and cautiously plodded to the coop, dreading what I might find. The hens were outside in the small fenced-in area under their house. They moved about nervously, pecking at a morsel here and there on the ground. Where was Brooster?

The yard was quiet. Too quiet. I stopped and looked around. Suddenly, just behind the coop I saw movement! A very large dark gray animal strutted back and forth. Its tail opened into a giant fan, then closed. Wings drooped. The whitish head turned and the long red snood shook with a "gobble-gobble-gobble." A tom turkey danced his courtship ritual for the chickens in the coop. He wanted to know my hens—-in the biblical sense!

A look inside the main coop revealed Brooster, cowering on the back roost. He had taken one look at that enormous bird and cackled, "You're on your own, girls!" Some protector!

When the gobbler saw me, he sauntered into the woods. Eventually, the lily-livered feathery wimp, Brooster, stuck his beak out to make sure the coast was clear.

Tonight when I opened the coop door to let the flock out to range, I told Brooster he was pathetic. "You are such a chicken!" I laughed at the pun and turned away. The hens clucked in agreement.

Just then, something sneaked up behind me. It crowed. It was Brooster, ready to attack.

Well, I guess it is good to know there are some things in life we can count on.

53

Think Coolness!

This week's weather forecast is enough to make one lose her cool. "Heat index up to 110..." The heat index is how hot it really FEELS when humidity is factored in with the actual air temperature. Just hearing the words "110 degrees" makes me FEEL hot. I immediately stalk to the refrigerator, dispense a glass of ice cubes into cold water and attempt to chill out.

Life was far different years ago when our parents grew up on the farm. Oh, it was plenty hot back then, too. They cut and stacked hay, harvested crops by hand and did chores in the hot South Dakota sun. This was before it was cool to know the temperature and heat index. Youngsters kept a cool head by holding it under the icy well water as they worked the pump handle.

Women cooked and baked in their farmhouse kitchens. All that hard work required energy. There were no refrigerators, no cold place to store leftovers. (This explains why families were so much larger back then; there couldn't be leftovers. Okay, that and the frigid South Dakota winters!) Giant blocks of ice remained frozen for a while in the ice house, but chipping off chunks was not cool. It was life: it was best to just play it cool and not complain.

So, years later when Mom and Dad married and had their own farm and two little ones, Mom thought it was the coolest thing ever when Dad brought home a refrigerator! Deloris remembers the small white Kelvinator with a pull-down handle. It had a tiny freezer compartment at the top just for ice cubes. Mom filled the aluminum ice cube trays with water and slid them into their special slots. Magic levers on the tops of the trays lifted to break and loosen the ice. In a few hours, frosty chipped squares were ready to cool a jar of lemonade to take to Dad in the field. How cool is that! Strawberry Jell-O became a refreshing summer treat.

A few years (and four kids) later, a bigger, better refrigerator adorned the kitchen. The freezer on top held lots more ice cube trays and a couple boxes of ice cream.

As the youngest and most spoiled child, I had no idea what it was like to do without a refrigerator or fans. "It's hot in here!" I announced after dinner one July day. My siblings gave me the "cool your jets!" look. I was sure there had to be some quick, easy way to cool off in the kitchen. "Can I use some ice cubes?" Mom nodded her permission. Cold air billowed out like a cloud when I opened the freezer door.

I twisted the flexible plastic trays over a cookie sheet. Cubes poured out to make a tiny ice mountain. I set the pan in front of the box fan and plopped down next to it. The chilly breeze from my wonderful invention made me feel cool as a cucumber!

The cubes melted. No one else was impressed.

Many years later on these hot sultry days in Iowa, I play Joe Cool. I put on my sunglasses and straw hat and head outside to pull some weeds, mow and do the chores. It FEELS really hot out there, so after a bit I slip inside to air-conditioned comfort. The side door on the fridge clunks out perfectly-formed ice cubes into my giant plastic glass. I chill out.

My life is like a soft summer breeze compared to my parents' growing up years. Still, I am thankful for air conditioning, refrigerators——and ice cubes!

Mom's Homemade Lemonade
   3-4 fresh lemons
   1 scant cup sugar

Cut lemons in half and squeeze in juicer. Dump juice, sugar and lemon rinds into a 2-quart jar. Fill half-full with cold water. Stir well. Add ice cubes and fill with water. Enjoy on a hot summer day when it FEELS like 110!

54

After-the-Game Entertainment

The year: 1962. The place: The Pheasant Bar, Winner, South Dakota. Seven young linemen sat in corner booths at the back. After a week of climbing power poles in the hot sun, they relaxed while conversations from two other tables carried across the room.

Two older guys shuffled in and settled on barstools. "Hey Ralph! Barney!" The bartender greeted them. "What happened? You two look like you just lost your mother!" The men just shook their heads in anguish, chins drooping to their chests.

More people ambled in——couples, families, teenagers——until nearly every booth and barstool was occupied. An aura of defeat loomed like a heavy cloud of smoke. The linemen watched and listened.

The throng was the after-game crowd. Tonight was the last in a four-game series, the Winner Pheasants against the Pierre Cowboys. The linemen were familiar with the baseball games. Winner was one of eight towns that comprised the Basin League. The townspeople supported their team with a passion.

In the last three weeks, the team of mostly college players hoping for a chance at the minor leagues, had moved from last place to second on the league roster. Excited players and fans held high expectations as the team met the Pierre Cowboys. Unfortunately, Pierre shot down the Pheasants' winning streak the first game, then blasted them in two more. So tonight the

Winner team desperately wanted a win.

The dialogue throughout the bar replayed the game. A home run brought in a runner in their first inning and the Pheasants scored two more in the fourth. Hopes soared. Stands rumbled under stomping feet.

The team kept their lead until the seventh inning. The Cowboys rallied with two hits. A wild pitch, steal and home run tied the game. The pitcher walked the next batter. The Pheasants felt hunted. The inning ended with the Pierre Cowboys ahead by two.

For the rest of the game the Cowboys kept the Pheasants corralled, allowing only two singles and striking out the last three batters in the ninth inning. Sorely disappointed, fans headed home or to local establishments like the Pheasant Bar.

Talk at the bar finally turned to the upcoming series with the Huron Jims. Hopes raised again for a winning streak. Fans finished their burgers and fries and headed home. The only people remaining were the linemen, four couples and Ralph and Barney.

The two old cronies lived and breathed baseball, reliving the days of their youth at each game. The bar chatter and their close proximity to the bartender finally ended their self-imposed silence.

"That pitcher shoulda pulled out a win. We had the lead, but he threw it away!" Barney's arm waved wildly in the air as he swiveled around to face his friend.

"Ha! You always blame the pitcher! As if YOU could do better!" Ralph plunked down his mug.

"I shore-nuff could! I got a good arm." Barney sputtered.

Ralph swiped Barney's spit off the side of his face and shook it off his hand disgustedly. "You couldn't throw ten feet!"

"Could too! Why...I could..." Barney thought. "I could throw clear over the Peacock!"

Ralph considered the location of the Peacock Bar, directly across the street. He laughed deliriously, hands clutching his stomach.

Perturbed at his friend's mocking, Barney struggled off his stool. "Somebody get me a baseball. I'll show you, Ralpphh."

A baseball was soon settled in Barney's hand. "Oh, boy! I can't wait to see thisss!" Ralph crowed. Every person in the bar, including the linemen, followed.

Outside, Barney stumbled backward as he blinked up, staring at the roof of the Peacock. He looked down at the baseball in his hand and swallowed.

"Wassa matter, Barney? Ya can't do it, can you?" Ralph almost fell over with all his laughing.

Barney stood as straight as he could at the moment, squared his shoulders, and wound up. He took a deep breath and lurched forward, hurling that baseball with all his might.

In a split second a clunk sounded, followed by the tinkling of breaking glass. Barney had put that baseball right through the window of the Peacock Bar!

The two old cronies gaped in shock. Finally, Ralph put his arm around Barney and they crossed the street.

The linemen grinned as they walked the two blocks to their hotel. They had missed the game, but they figured they had the best entertainment of the night.

(Thanks to one of those seven linemen who told me the story about the night at the Pheasant Bar back in 1962 in Winner, S.D.)

<h1 style="text-align:center">55</h1>

Barefoot in the Thistle Patch

On the top of my right foot there is a small triangle-shaped scar. Scars usually have stories to tell. I wish I could remember a fierce fight with a savage gopher or raccoon, but I only recall hoeing thistles in the cornfield with Delmer. Since our brains choose what we remember, my guess is the scar resulted from a slight miscalculation on my part. And being barefoot.

My siblings and I all remember hoeing thistles. Deloris and Don were not very old when they scampered behind Mom and Dad through the corn rows. The youngsters did their best to chop out the thorny plants and the folks patiently covered any they missed. Deloris says it was hot, dirty work.

Every year when the corn was about knee-high, Dad sharpened our garden hoes in preparation for the war. The cultivator eradicated the weeds between the rows, but hoes and strong backs fought the culprits encroaching on the corn plants. The enemy grew in patches, so we rode on the back of the tractor (Delmer remembers Don driving the John Deere 730 with the cultivator attached.) to the next patch. Sometimes the cluster was so big we had to work frantically to wipe them out before Don came back, cultivating the next four rows.

One summer day I was riding with Dad in the pickup. As usual, he drove with his tanned elbow sticking out the rolled-down window, checking the crops. All at once, he spun the pickup into the approach next to the south cornfield. Dad hopped out and headed for a spot in the end rows. He reached down and pulled out several three foot plants and threw them on the ground. I gasped as I realized he was pulling prickly thistles!

The dreadful scourge we battled back then on our South Dakota farm was the Canada thistle. It is a perennial species of flowering plant, native to Europe and western Asia. It spreads aggressively by roots and seeds and it blooms with a distinctive fuzzy purple flower. Scientific name: Cirsium arvense. Curse describes it perfectly in my opinion!

Childhood lessons stick with us in this life, so I have spent the last 20 years chopping thistles, Canada thistle, sow thistle—every thistle I find.

Last week at a Master Conservationist program on prairie plants, I made the unnerving discovery that there is a GOOD thistle! Seriously! One thistle growing here in Iowa is a native of the tallgrass prairies that covered the state years ago. It is the Tall Thistle. Unlike the Canada thistle, it is not invasive. This plant is beneficial for butterflies, bees and songbirds. The Goldfinch, a strict vegetarian, relies on seeds for its diet. Finches love Tall Thistle, and will perch on the top and happily dine on the seeds all winter long.

It wasn't easy, but I needed to change my strategy in the thistle war. Now when I head to the yard with my trusty hoe, I stop before I chop. I determine whether that thorny plant might be a good thistle. AND, I wear boots!

56

Walk Boldly and Carry a Big Corn Knife

Rough dark leaves grazed my face and arms and made me itch. Toes sank into the black South Dakota dirt as I trudged between rows of tall fibrous stalks. At the top of each stalk, light brown growth protruded like a miniature tree with thin, arm-like branches. Tiny yellow grains clung to each rough branch and fell as we brushed by. A distinctive odor hung in the thick air, growing more intense as we moved. Not a breath of breeze penetrated the thick, hot jungle around us.

The jungle was the cornfield just north of the shelter belt. The corn was in tassel. The yellow grains were pollen, which emitted the characteristic sweet-and-sour odor.

Dad had sent Mom, Delmer and me to eliminate the sunflowers that had evaded the cultivator. Mom commandeered the middle. Delmer covered the two rows to her left. They wielded corn knives. (I was not allowed a corn knife, possibly because of the hoe incident.) Every ten yards or so, I heard one of them chop once, maybe twice, as another formidable foe bit the dust. I pulled the smaller plants in my row and called to Mom to bring down the more sizeable scoundrels.

Dorothy was not very old when Dad handed her a corn knife. "Go up and down the corn rows and chop down all the sunflowers." She knew what sunflowers were, so she headed for the field. She chopped away for what seemed like the whole day. A few days later when Donald cultivated, he came home, chuckling about the sunflowers that weren't chopped below the bottom leaves and would just grow back. Dad did not say a word, but in my mind I can see him shake his head and grin just a little, realizing that his little girl had simply followed his instructions.

Sunflowers were not welcome anywhere on our South Dakota farm. I once asked Dad why sunflowers were bad. He replied that they were hard on the combine. And they showed up everywhere! So we hoed them out of end rows, pulled them when they dared to show their ugly heads under the windmill and chopped them out of fields and pastures. At an early age, we learned to hate those tall weeds with the yellow flowers that sought the sun.

Memories stick with us, good or bad, whether we want them or not. Today, when I see a florist bouquet bedecked with five colors of sunflowers, I wrinkle my nose in quiet disdain.

The last issue of my favorite garden catalog devoted one full glossy photo page to sunflowers—thirteen various varieties! I glanced over them, (obviously counted), and read a few of the blurbs. Butterflies love them. They come in every size and color imaginable. They are lovely in containers.

Hmph! I flipped the page. I cannot, I will not purchase any plant that is even slightly related to that dreaded plague of my youth!

Okay, maybe next year...

57

It's Not Just About the Ribbons

"It's time to get up, DeAnn! There's a lot to do this morning," Mom called up the stairs. The tone of her voice indicated that this morning she would not be my snooze button. Sleep webs slowly cleared from my brain and I realized what day it was—the first day of county fair!

It was late last night when I glued the final touches on my safety poster. Covered with plastic, it waited on the kitchen table with the other exhibits that Delmer and I were taking to the fair. Kingsbury County called the event Achievement Days. 4-H'ers and others brought their best livestock, crafts, garden produce, and canned and baked goods to be judged. Each place was awarded a ribbon. First place received a purple ribbon. Then there was blue, red and white. Everyone hoped for a purple. A purple ribbon meant you got to take that item to the state fair in Huron.

Today was entry day. Mom, Dad and Delmer were already outside getting the chickens ready. We had caught them last night using a flashlight to find the best looking ones on the roosts. This morning the young birds chattered softly in the metal cage, wondering what was in store for them. Delmer picked out what he thought was the best rooster. Dad held the Plymouth Rock by both feet while Delmer cleaned off any dirt. When the cockerel was Saturday-night-clean, my brother rubbed olive oil over its comb, wattles and feet.

It was my turn. Dad held the hen I chose. I cleaned and oiled her until she shined in the morning sun. "Are you gonna win me a purple ribbon?" I petted

158

her one last time before Dad and Delmer put the cages in the pickup.

Mom and I headed for the barn. Mom put an arm on my shoulder. "It's not just the ribbon, you know. It's what you learn that is important."

The dress on the table labeled as a clothing exhibit flashed through my mind. Though our mother had the patience of Job, I wonder if she wished her youngest had been a boy. The fifth time I had to get out the seam ripper, I was fit to be tied. I kept sewing the facing into the neck seam. I learned a lot sewing that red swirly-print dress. I learned I would never do that again!

Delmer and I dragged several hog panels into place to make an aisle for the pigs from the barn to the water tank. We probably didn't need the panels anymore, but on fair day we didn't want to be chasing our pigs around the yard. Two months ago we gave our 4-H hogs their first bath. They squealed like crazy and tried to jump out. After the third time, they learned to love bath time. They closed their eyes, lifted their noses and grunted contentedly as we brushed soap and water through their bristly coats. Delmer scrubbed his Duroc boar first and put him back into a pristine pen. Two gilts came out next. My brother and I would compete against each other in this class.

Delmer had won the showmanship trophy last year. As we scrubbed our dark red hogs who thought they were in hog heaven, he gave me tips for the show ring. "Never get between your hog and the judge. Keep your eye on him while you guide your pig so he can see her best points."

I told my brother I didn't figure I had a chance for showmanship, but I sure wanted a purple ribbon on my hog. Dad came along about then and watched our piggy spa. "You two know the ribbon and the trophy are not the important part. No matter who wins, you be a good sport."

Images of show ring glories danced in our heads. Dad knew what we were thinking. "You make sure and congratulate the winner. Look them in the eye like you mean it. Shake their hand. That will make me prouder than anything."

As it turned out, Delmer and I were both happy with the results that day. And I think Dad and Mom were pretty proud, too. Even though they brought us up to know what was truly important, they were about as happy to see a purple ribbon as we were!

58

Picking, Grinning and Shelling

Eight greedy beasts roamed the ground below me, watching...waiting. Like ravenous vultures they circled, ready to pounce on anything that dropped to the ground. When something did they raced to the spot. The winner grabbed it in her sharp beak and gobbled it down.

The beasts were part of my flock, a menagerie of normally gentle hens of every age and color. I sat in my favorite evening spot in front of the chicken coops, shelling peas. Occasionally a pea landed in the grass and the girls scrambled for it.

I split a crisp green pod with my thumbnail and peeled it open. Eight little green orbs plunked into the stainless steel bowl. The sound reminded me of shelling peas around the kitchen table when I was a little girl.

It was early July. Mom had planted three long rows of Little Marvel that spring and they were ready to be picked. She and her daughters moved down the rows, stooping to lift the vines and pluck off the plump pods. She kept an eye on us to make sure we didn't tear the plant. "Hold on just above the pod when you pull it off," she instructed. "If you don't break the vine there will be more pickings." As our buckets filled, we learned that we should never pick when the plants are wet, since that spreads disease.

Many hands make light work. It wasn't long until we lugged four heaping pails into the house and dumped them in the middle of the kitchen table. Each of us found a bowl and sat down next to the green mountain. The pails waited on the floor to hold the empty pods. The sounds of shells tearing and peas dropping into bowls surrounded us.

Dad came in from the Quonset. He and the boys were getting the combine ready for oats. He smiled at his girls and pulled another chair up. "Good crop!" Mom beamed proudly. Dorothy hurried to bring more empty bowls as Donald and Delmer walked in.

All eight of us worked on that green mountain that day, our mouths watering at the prospect of fresh peas and new potatoes for supper. Suddenly we heard something hit the floor, bounce and roll. Mom laughed and told us her brothers' story from a few summers back. They had the brilliant idea of using the wringer on the washing machine to shell their peas. "They flew all over the kitchen!" We pictured peas shooting every direction as the wringer squeezed the pods. "They just swept them up when they were done. Ma didn't think much of it." We envisioned our little grandma with the white bun on top of her head brushing peas off her stove and every other surface.

The mountain on our table quickly morphed to one large kettle of peas for supper, a big porcelain bowlful to can for winter and several buckets of empty pods the boys hauled to the pigs.

The chickens wandered off as I finished shelling my own measly half-bucket and looked down at the bowl in my lap. Two meals and a few to eat raw.

I shook my head, wondering if a couple bowls of peas was worth all the work and the garden space. Should I even bother with them next year? I thought of our mother and I knew such a thought would never have entered her mind.

Eventually the girls found roosts in their respective coops and I tucked them in for the night. I carried the precious bowl of peas to the house and cooked them. A wonderful smell filled the kitchen as I turned off the burner. I poured in a bit of half-and-half because that's the way Mom made them.

I closed my eyes and savored that first spoonful of heavenly bliss. And I remembered.

Next year I might even plant two rows!

Deloris, Don, Dorothy and Darlene

59

Zero to Eight in Sixty

Imagine every pair of shoes you have ever worn lined up in chronological order. Each pair clutches a story unleashed by memories. Baby feet kicked off size zero booties knitted by an aunt. Doctors recommended sturdy leather shoes for toddlers. "They need support when they begin to walk!"

Feet grew so fast many pairs appeared in our lineups. Maybe there were hand-me-downs, scuffed and threadbare. Shiny patent leathers worn only once as a flower girl or ring-bearer? Were there slippers scrunched flat from wear, with holes in the toes?

When a friend got sparkly play heels for her birthday, of course I begged Mom for some. She told me to find a pair of my sisters' old ones in the closet. The resulting dress-up play proved far more valuable to the imagination than flimsy elastic straps glued to glittery plastic, though I didn't know it then.

Some shoes symbolized coming-of-age. Delmer remembers when Dad took him to the shoe store in De Smet to buy his first pair of work boots. When the young boy stepped into those boots he felt empowered; now he was big enough to be a farmer just like Dad and Donald.

Girls couldn't wait to wear heels, but sometimes mothers felt that prom was soon enough. Pointy toes and round toes have come and gone several times in our lifetime.

As hemlines went up, shoes grew more important in wardrobes. After WWII leather became readily available and manufacturers pumped out more styles

163

and colors than ever just for our generation! We wore black and white saddle shoes which were a challenge to polish. For good luck we tucked pennies in penny loafers. We wore pumps, sandals and mules. Flip-flops slapped into our heels as we walked. (Can you believe we called them thongs?)

Bright white tennis shoes made us feel like cheerleaders, even if we weren't. I recall sponging white liquid polish on mine when one shoe got a scuff mark.

Nancy Sinatra claimed her "go-go boots" were made for walking, but no shoes made us want to walk a mile as much as comfy athletic shoes now available in neon colors!

In a recent radio talk show the hosts wanted listeners to call in and tell about their shoes. The radio people claimed that psychologists today can tell about our personality by what we have on our feet.

Are the heels of your dress shoes worn on the outside, but you keep wearing them? Do you scrunch your feet into a size-too-small stiletto like Cinderella's wicked stepsisters? Is there a nick in the right toe of your work boot where the hoe somehow missed the relentless poison ivy vine? Do you continue to wear your favorite size-eight athletic shoes even though they are worn and dirty? Does a distinctive odor fill the room when you kick off those sneakers?

Hmmmm. I think I'm glad I don't know any psychologists at the moment. However, if I knew I was going to see one, I would buy a new pair of shoes!

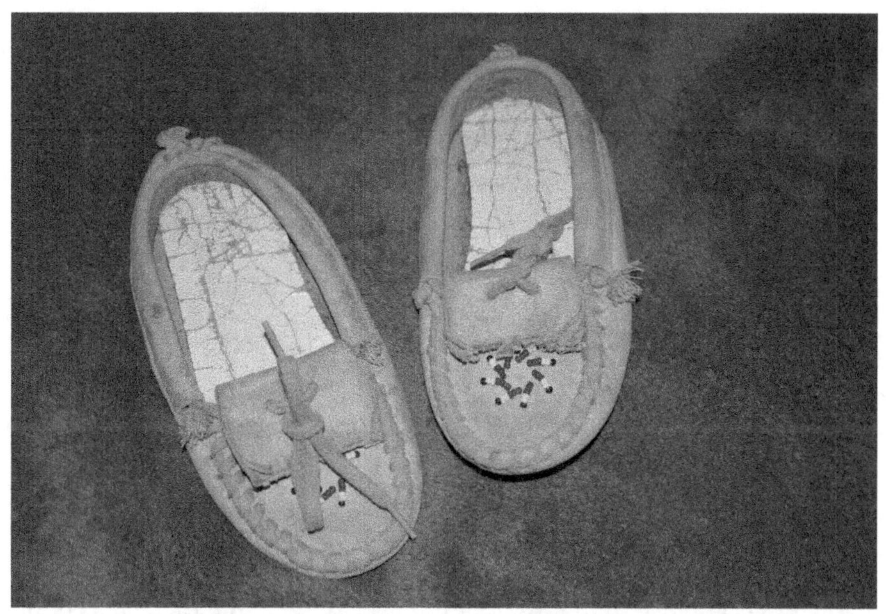

DeAnn's moccasins purchased in the Black Hills.

60

A Time to Shine

Sundays, weddings and funerals. Two things were cleaned and polished for those special days: the car and our shoes. Weather permitting, someone parked the car close to the front yard fence. With an old rag and a couple buckets of hot soapy water, Dad or the kids washed it, top to bottom. Mom brought out the chamois and a fresh pail of water and we polished that car to a spot-free sparkle.

The folks took pride in their family's appearance, but I am pretty sure another important factor was their desire to take care of what we had. Things were harder to come by then, and it was important to make them last. Shoes also stood high on the priority list.

The shoe kit was kept in a small cabinet in the kitchen. The box contained various bottles and metal canisters of polishes in liquid, wax, or crème boasting the brands "Kiwi," and "Esquire." There were two soft, polish-infused rags that smelled wonderful, maybe of carnauba or lanolin.

The boys occasionally applied a leather conditioner to their work boots to keep them water-proof. After all, if you had a good pair of boots you wanted them to last a while. Sometimes Dad took boots to a shoe shop in Huron. The cobbler could replace a worn-down sole or put in new hooked eyelets for just a few dollars.

Mom happily shined Dad's dress shoes, but it was us kids' job to take care of our own. The bottles of liquid polish had a sponge applicator on the top. It was fun to watch the black or white polish soak into the shoe surface.

Delmer remembers when a bottle of shoe polish nearly got him into trouble. It was Saturday and we were all scurrying about, getting ready for a wedding. Deloris, Lowell and their little girl, Susan had spent the night. Susan toddled around in a frilly white dress, grinning happily as we told her how cute she was. It was soon time to leave for the church when Delmer walked into the kitchen in perfectly pressed white shirt and gray pants. He stepped into his dress shoes and noticed scuff marks on the toes. Quickly, he grabbed the shoe kit, pulled out the bottle of black liquid polish and sponged it over the shoes. He put the kit away and waited.

In the next few minutes of hustle and bustle, no one knew what happened, but somehow splotches of black shoe polish appeared on the front of Susan's beautiful white dress! Deloris scrambled to scrub the stains out of the dress. Miraculously, the black marks came out, leaving no evidence of the near-calamity that had occurred. There were a few tense moments when the folks likely wanted to tan Delmer's hide, but no one figured out how the polish got on the dress. My brother was innocent (this time).

Times are different now. I do not own one container of any kind of shoe polish. I replace my go-to athletic shoes when the soles get worn. Shoes I no longer wear are hauled to a donation center. Not once do I consider shining them or keeping them nice.

As I write this, my thoughts amble to an old photo of our parents. They are standing proudly in front of their sparkly-clean Ford Galaxy on a bright Sunday morning. I can still picture the stylish hats on their heads and smiles on their faces. And I remember their shoes. Likely those shoes had traveled a few miles and plodded through some hard times. But like the car, they still shined like brand-new.

Mom and the kids and the sparkly-clean car. Dorothy, Deloris, Darlene, Donald, Delmer, DeAnn and Mom.

Also by DeAnn (Wolkow) Kruempel

The author has published six books: a previous book of short stories, *Once Upon a Midwest Sunset* and a series of five historical fiction books, the *Promises to Keep* series. Every book is loved by readers of all ages!

Once Upon a Midwest Sunset Stories from the Nooks and Crannies Collection printed in several Midwest newspapers in 2020-2021. Many relate memories of growing up on the family's South Dakota farm. They will make you laugh, cry and remember your own stories.

Promises to Keep Series
  Promises to Keep
  Promises Challenged
  Promises Strengthened
  Promises in Courage
  Promises Under Fire

All are available at Amazon.com